a 684311   J 394. 2663 World

W9-ALJ-936

a 684311   J 394. 2663 World

Christmas in
PUERTO RICO

Christmas Around the World
from World Book

World Book, Inc.
a Scott Fetzer company

Chicago

Staff

President and Publisher
Robert C. Martin

Vice President, Editorial
Dominic J. Miccolis

Editor in Chief
Dale Jacobs

General Managing Editor, World Book Publishing
Paul A. Kobasa

Editorial

Managing Editor, General Publishing and Annuals
Maureen Mostyn Liebenson

Associate Editor
Shawn Brennan

Writer
Lisa Klobuchar

Manager, Cartographic Services
Wayne K. Pichler

Permissions Editor
Janet T. Peterson

Head, Indexing Services
David Pofelski

Manager, Research Services
Loranne K. Shields

Staff Researcher
Anel Méndez Velázquez

Art

Manager, Graphics and Design
Sandra Dyrlund

Senior Designer
Isaiah Sheppard

Contributing Photographs Editor
Kathryn Creech

Production and Administrative Assistant
John Whitney

Production

Director, Manufacturing and Pre-Press
Carma Fazio

Manager, Manufacturing
Barbara Podczerwinski

Senior Production Manager
Madelyn Underwood

Print Promotional Manager
Marco Morales

Proofreader
Anne Dillon

Text Processing
Gwendolyn Johnson

J 394.2 CHRISTMAS
Christmas in Puerto Rico.
30405090684679 New Milford Public
Library Dec 1 2005

World Book wishes to thank the following for their contributions to Christmas in Puerto Rico: Karen Zack Ingebretsen, Francisco dePadua Morales, Emilie Schrage, and the Institute of Puerto Rican Culture.

© 2004 World Book, Inc. All rights reserved. This volume may not be reproduced in whole or in part in any form without prior written permission from the publisher. WORLD BOOK is a registered trademark or trademark of World Book, Inc.

Every effort has been made to locate copyright holders of material in this volume.

World Book, Inc.
233 N. Michigan Avenue
Chicago, IL 60601

For information about other World Book publications, visit our Web site **http://www.worldbook.com**, or call **1-800-WORLDBK (967-5325)**. For information about sales to schools and libraries, call **1-800-975-3250 (United States); 1-800-837-5365 (Canada)**.

Library of Congress Cataloging-in-Publication Data
Christmas in Puerto Rico.
    p. cm. — (Christmas around the world from World Book)
    Summary: Describes the traditions and customs that are part of the celebration of Christmas in Puerto Rico as well as presenting crafts, recipes, and songs.
    Includes index.
    ISBN 0-7166-0801-4
            1. Christmas—Puerto Rico—Juvenile literature. 2. Puerto Rico—Social life and customs—Juvenile literature. [1. Christmas—Puerto Rico. 2. Puerto Rico—Social life and customs.] I. World Book, Inc. II. Series.

GT4987.28 .C47 2004
394.2663'097295—dc21
                                    2003008726

Printed in Malaysia
2 3 4 5 6 7 8 9 10 09 08 07 06 05

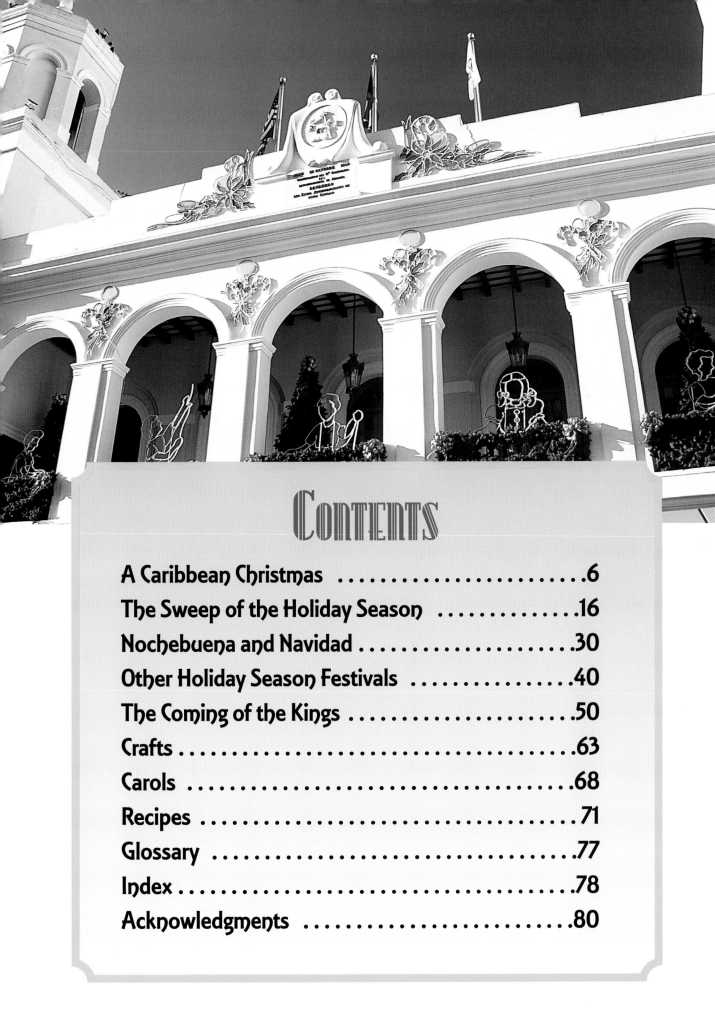

Contents

A Caribbean Christmas

I n Puerto Rico, the sights, scents, and sounds of Christmas are wrapped in warm tropical breezes: tiny lights winking among swaying palm fronds . . . the mouth-watering aroma of slow-roasting pork competing with the perfume of exotic blossoms . . . joyous voices raised in song accompanied by guitar and maracas.

When Christopher Columbus landed in Puerto Rico in 1493, it was inhabited by the Taíno Indians. The Taínos called their island *Borikén,* which means "Great Land of the Valiant and Noble Lord," and Puerto Ricans still like to refer to their homeland as *Borinquen.* Columbus claimed the island for Spain and named it San Juan Bautista (St. John the Baptist). In the early colonial days, *Puerto Rico,* which means *rich port* in Spanish, was the name for San Juan, the island's capital and largest city. The name gradually came to be used for the entire island.

San Juan is Puerto Rico's capital and largest city. Modern hotels and condominiums line the city's shore.

The Spanish ruled Puerto Rico for some 400 years, infusing the island with their Catholicism, their architecture, their government, and, especially, their language. Slaves from West Africa, brought to work the sugar cane fields, added their spirituality, food, and music. Since 1898, Puerto Rico has been a

Opposite page:
Old San Juan, with its charming cobblestone streets, pastel buildings, and wrought-iron balconies, sparkles with lights at night.

Puerto Rico is a roughly rectangular island that lies between the North Atlantic Ocean and the Caribbean Sea. It is southeast of the mainland of the United States.

Puerto Rico's flag was designed about 1895 and was officially adopted in 1952. On the seal, the lamb symbolizes peace and brotherhood. The letters *F* and *I* stand for King Ferdinand and Queen Isabella of Spain.

possession of the United States. All these cultures have blended to create the colorful fabric of Puerto Rican life. Its Christmas traditions are no exception.

Puerto Rico, a little jewel of an island in the Caribbean, is the smallest member of the island group known as the Greater Antilles (which also includes Cuba, Jamaica, and Hispaniola [comprised of Haiti and the Dominican Republic]). It is also the most easterly island of the group. Located 1,000 miles southeast of Florida, Puerto Rico measures 100 miles from east to west and 35 miles from north to south. It is a roughly rectangular island, with many of its largest cities—San Juan, Ponce, Mayagüez, Aguadilla, and Arecibo—arrayed around the coastal areas. It is one of the most densely populated places on Earth.

The Greater Antilles lie on the border between the North Atlantic Ocean and the Caribbean Sea. The climate can be described as uniformly pleasant, with average temperatures hovering around 80 °F the year around, bright sun, and refreshing sea breezes. The island's varied landscape features sandy beaches, steaming rain forests, and 4,000-foot-high mountains where coffee is grown. Except for tropical birds, wildlife does not abound in Puerto Rico. There are no large mammals and only a handful of reptile species. A small tree frog—called the coquí for its musical two-note call, *koh-kee, koh-kee* (which musicians will recognize as a perfect seventh)—is something of a national mascot. Poinsettias, the holiday plant beloved the world over, grow 10 feet tall there in a profusion of vivid red and green.

San Juan lies toward the eastern end of the northern coast. The oldest city "under the U.S. flag" was founded in 1511 by Juan Ponce de León. The historical heart of the city is *El Viejo San Juan,* or Old San Juan, the original walled settlement. Old San Juan comprises seven square blocks of colonial architecture. The pastel houses that line the cobblestone streets are never more charming than at Christmastime, when wrought-iron balconies are decorated with lights, bows, pine wreaths and garlands, and poinsettias.

A mix of cultures

When the Spanish established settlements on Puerto Rico around 1500, the native inhabitants, the Taíno, maintained a well-developed culture made up of about 20 villages ruled by a single chief. Their religious system was complex, based on a hierarchy of sky gods. The Taíno were skilled farmers, sailors, and fishermen. Anthropologists can only guess at their population at the time of the Spaniards' arrival, but it may have been as many as 50,000.

The Spanish originally colonized the island to mine for gold. For several decades, Spanish entrepreneurs, supported by Indian slave labor, were able to grow rich in the gold mining industry. But the mines were depleted by 1540, and the

The coquí sounds a clear, musical note during the evening hours on the island. The little tree frog is something of a national mascot for Puerto Rico.

El Morro Fortress stands on a bluff overlooking the Bay of San Juan. Spaniards built the fort between 1539 and 1787.

The Cordillera Central mountain range stretches across south-central Puerto Rico. The island's highest peak, Cerro de Punta, rises 4,389 feet in the range. Farmers grow coffee and many kinds of citrus fruits in the region's fertile valleys.

Spanish needed to find another source of revenue. Sugar was in demand in Europe, and the colonists soon found that the climate in Puerto Rico was perfect for growing sugar cane. Large plantations sprung up in the valleys and lowlands along the coasts. However, the traditional labor source, the Taínos, had by this time been almost entirely wiped out by disease, warfare, and ill-treatment by their Spanish masters. The Spanish began importing blacks from West Africa as their new slave-labor pool.

Many Taíno traditions live on to this day, including their hanging bed, the *hamaca,* which English-speakers call a hammock; *barbacoa,* or barbecue; and the rhythm instruments the *güiro* and the *maracas,* which play such a special role in the music of the holiday season in Puerto Rico. Another reminder of the Taíno is in the name of the type of fierce tropical storm that these people called a *hurakán.*

The jíbaro

Some of the few surviving Indians, along with *mestizos* (people of mixed Spanish and Indian or black ancestry), fled to the mountains and scratched out a meager living growing cassava (a plant with edible starchy roots), corn, rice, and other crops. These peasant mountain folk became known as *jíbaros.*

Many Puerto Ricans wistfully consider the culture of the jíbaro their true spiritual as well as national identity. Puerto Ricans adore the jíbaro soul in their modern culture much as mainland Americans cherish their tales and heroes of the Old West. The traditional image of the jíbaro is of a tiller of the soil, poor but proud; illiterate, but with a homespun wisdom. A natural musician and storyteller, feet bare and head covered by the typical straw hat called the *pava,* the jíbaro is seen as independent, self-sufficient, gracious to visitors, and resourceful. A cultural identity based on the jíbaro has grown up around the image of this figure. Certain styles of music, dance, turns of speech, jokes, and folk tales are understood by Puerto Ricans as "jíbaro."

At Christmastime, the essence of the jíbaro is evident as Puerto Ricans don pavas, pick up their 10-stringed *cuatros,* shake their maracas, and gather for the singing of Puerto Rican Christmas carols called *aguinaldos.*

Roman Catholicism

Long rule by the Spanish made Roman Catholicism the chief religion of Puerto Rico. Its influence is felt the year around in the saints' festivals that abound in Puerto Rico. Christmas masses and *Nacimientos,* or Nativity scenes, are a treasured part of the holiday observance. Some Nacimientos and the figures that populate them are created by master woodcarvers called *santeros,* who specialize in figures of saints called *santos.* In a typically Puerto Rican blend of cultural traditions, a Nacimiento carved by renowned santero Pablo Rinaldi Jovet features the Baby Jesus slumbering peacefully in a hammock.

Many Puerto Ricans consider the culture of the jíbaro their true spiritual as well as national identity.

Dressed in traditional costumes, Puerto Ricans celebrate holidays with colorful festivals that feature traditional music, dancing, and parades.

Puerto Rican dancers perform folk dances in Ponce.

The 51st state?

The Commonwealth of Puerto Rico, as it's officially known, is a possession of the United States. Puerto Ricans are U.S. citizens and can travel freely to the mainland. However, they cannot vote in presidential elections while they are on the island. They do not pay federal income taxes. Puerto Rico was a war prize for the United States, won, along with the Philippines, from Spain after its defeat in the Spanish-American War in 1898. In 1917, Puerto Ricans were granted U.S. citizenship. Local officials were elected by the people. As a colony, the island's chief executive, the governor, was appointed by the American president. Until 1946, all the governors were Anglos from the mainland. At that time, the United States granted Puerto

Ricans the right to choose their own governor.

In 1950, under U.S. President Harry S. Truman, Puerto Ricans were offered the opportunity to decide whether to make the switch in status from colony to commonwealth. As a commonwealth, the United States would retain political control over Puerto Rico, but the citizens would have the power to draw up their own constitution. They voted overwhelmingly in 1951 for commonwealth status.

From the beginning of U.S. domination, Puerto Rico had an independence movement. Sometimes those who passionately believed that Puerto Rico should be an independent country expressed their belief through violence. But the movement never took hold among the population as a whole. Having established commonwealth status, the Puerto Ricans had three levels of relationship with the United States to choose from: They could make their connection closer by becoming a state. They could retain their commonwealth status. Or they could sever the relationship and become an independent nation. During the lead-up to a second vote on the issue in 1967, the popular former governor Luis Muñoz Marín laid out the arguments in favor of remaining a commonwealth. Statehood, on the one hand, would preserve and enhance the economically beneficial relationship with the United States, but it would threaten Puerto Rico's unique culture. Independence would certainly preserve Puerto Rico's culture, but, Muñoz Marín argued, the economic benefits of a close alliance with the United States would be lost. The voters agreed and Puerto Rico remained a commonwealth.

From the beginning of U.S. domination, Puerto Rico had an independence movement.

Today, the debate continues. The *Partido Nuevo Progresista* supports Puerto Rican statehood. Its most vociferous opponent, the *Partido Independentista Puertorriqueño,* wants independence. In the middle, with the most popular support, is the *Partido Popular Democrático.* Its "leave well enough alone" point of view continues to hold sway, and in a popular vote in 1993, Puerto Ricans again chose to remain a commonwealth. They reaffirmed this position in 1998, demonstrating that at least for the time being Puerto Ricans were content to remain somewhat distant relatives of the United States.

The Christmas tree is an acquired holiday tradition in Puerto Rico. A beautifully decorated Christmas tree adorns a courtyard in San Juan's Plaza Las Américas, one of the largest malls in Latin America.

Hand in hand with the United States

So many people travel back and forth between Puerto Rico and the United States that it is hardly surprising that Puerto Ricans there have adopted many mainland Christmas traditions.

The U.S. influence shows up in many ways during the holiday season. U.S. Christmas carols are so popular that, although the tropical island has never experienced a frost—let alone snow—Puerto Ricans can be heard singing about the joys of "dashing through the snow in a one-horse open sleigh" in the popular Christmas song "Cascabel," or "Jingle Bells." Or they may admit, musically, of dreaming of a white Christmas in "Blanca Navidad," their translation of Irving Berlin's classic.

Another acquired tradition at Christmastime is the Christmas tree. Every year, thousands of trees are shipped from growers in the United States and Canada. Puerto Ricans decorate the trees at home with lights and ornaments. In addition, cities put up large trees in their plazas, or town squares. Ponce, Puerto Rico's second-largest city, broke a Puerto Rican Christmas-tree size record in 1998 when it imported a 62-foot-tall, 34-foot-wide, 7-ton behemoth. This giant tree was shipped by barge from Pennsauken, New Jersey.

And as on the mainland, Puerto Ricans do their Christmas shopping with diligence. At Christmastime, the Plaza Las Américas in San Juan, one of the largest malls in Latin America—and one of the world's leaders in sales—is jammed with people looking not only for gifts for Christmas but for Three Kings Day as well.

"Feliz Navidad"

"Feliz Navidad" by Puerto Rican native José Feliciano has become a Christmas classic.

In 1998, to commemorate the 85th anniversary of its founding, the American Society of Composers, Authors, and Publishers (ASCAP) named its "Top 25 Holiday Songs of the Century." Weighing in at number 14 was "Feliz Navidad," by Grammy-award winning Puerto Rican native son José Feliciano. The simple but catchy song has become a Christmas classic.

Compared with other songs on the list, which paint detailed landscapes of the holiday season, telling stories, re-creating a holiday mood filled with nostalgic longing, the appeal of "Feliz Navidad" is in its pure, joyful simplicity. Made up of only three statements—"Feliz Navidad," "Próspero año y felicidad," and "I wanna wish you a Merry Christmas from the bottom of my heart"—repeated for three minutes over a jangly guitar and a brass accompaniment, the song has been a worldwide favorite since it was released in 1970.

The song, ironically, was written in the summer, while Feliciano and his producer were working on a Christmas album. The producer suggested that it might be a good idea for Feliciano to write an original tune for the album. As Feliciano recalled the togetherness of the holiday gatherings in his large family (he was 1 of 11 boys), "Feliz Navidad" practically developed in a matter of minutes.

Feliciano plays guitar, bass, percussion and, of course, the 10-stringed guitarlike cuatro on the recording, and performs both lead and background vocals. The song became the most popular track on the album and since its first appearance, it has been recorded by many artists, including Céline Dion and the Three Tenors (José Carreras, Plácido Domingo, and Luciano Pavarotti).

The original *Billboard* magazine review, which appeared in November 1970, remarked on the "interesting new dimensions" that Feliciano added to Christmas favorites such as "Silent Night," "The Little Drummer Boy," and "The Cherry Tree Carol." Interestingly, no mention was made of "Feliz Navidad," the little tune that would create a holiday sensation and remain a cherished fixture in the world's holiday songbook for years to come.

The Sweep of the Holiday Season

The influence of the United States has given Puerto Ricans a convenient day to kick off their long holiday season—the day after Thanksgiving. The holiday season merrily skips on for weeks here, all the way to the third week in January in some households. Puerto Ricans work hard at having fun at Christmastime, but they make it look so easy.

Opposite page: Paseo La Princesa in Old San Juan hosts a traditional holiday show called *"Paseo de Luz,"* or "Promenade of Light" each year at Christmastime.

The Christmas trees go up. Lights are strung on homes, streets, public buildings, cactuses, palm trees, and other tropical foliage. Even the former city dump in San Juan— long since filled to capacity— sparkles with the greeting *"Feliz Navidad."* Nativity scenes are assembled in homes, churches, and public places throughout the island. Cooks at home and in public restaurants begin concocting the traditional Christmas favorites, and holiday activities known as *parrandas* begin.

San Juan City Hall lights up at night during Christmas season in Puerto Rico.

Music is so much a part of what it means to be Puerto Rican that it is no surprise that it's pretty much everywhere you direct your ears during the holiday season. In Puerto Rico, though, music is much more than what's piped through the sound systems of stores to soothe hurried shoppers.

When it comes to music, Puerto Ricans really participate. Families gathered on patios or balconies may begin a spontaneous holiday concert. People supplied with sheet music and accompanied by traditional instruments may join a caroling group in a city plaza or park, or before one of the many public Nativity scenes. But the most important venue for holiday music making is the parranda.

No rest for the merry

The parranda is a unique form of holiday activity that arises naturally from the Puerto Rican love of music, food, and fellowship. During a parranda, groups of singers and musicians, often called *trullas,* assemble and go from house to house singing Christmas carols.

According to custom, when a trulla comes a-caroling to your home, usually at 10 or 11 o'clock at night, you are obliged to reward its members with a treat. This might be a glass of *coquito,* the traditional holiday drink, which is sort of a coconut eggnog. For grown-ups, it's fortified with rum, for which Puerto Rico is famous. Or the trulla might be offered a tamalelike *pastel,* or a Spanish nougat. It's not so much the treat that counts but the camaraderie and the sharing. Often, the hosts join the trulla for its visit to the next house, so the group grows ever larger as the night goes on.

A parranda may take a special form, called an *asalto,* or assault. This surprise musical attack occurs in the middle of the night, when a trulla shows up at somebody's home, yells *"Asalto!"* and begins to belt out a song. Whether the occupants are awake or asleep, they are expected to receive the group warmly. There are two ways to prepare for such surprise attacks. One is to keep a supply of Christmas goodies on hand. The other—less festive but very effective when a decent night's sleep is a necessity—is to park your car down the street, turn off all the lights, and hope the trulla will think no one is home.

> The most important venue for holiday music making is the parranda.

Some parranderos plan their evening to end up at a certain house. This visit is never a surprise for the hosts—even though it may occur at four or five in the morning—because it's their job to prepare a big pot of *sopón de pollo con arroz,* or chicken soup with rice to eat at the end of the evening.

Parranda music

Trullas usually include one or more guitarlike instruments. Chief among them is the 10-stringed cuatro. The cuatro, whose bright sound resembles a cross between a 12-stringed guitar and a mandolin, has become a symbol of Puerto Rican cultural identity. The cuatro looks

During a parranda, groups of singers and musicians, often called trullas, assemble and go from house to house singing Christmas carols.

Don Alejandro Lozado is a well-known artisan of güiros. These percussion instruments are made from the long, gourdlike fruit of the higuero tree.

almost anyone. Maracas and güiros both have their roots in the Taíno Indian culture. Traditionally, maracas were a pair of dried, hollowed-out round gourds called *higueras* filled with dried beans, seeds, or pebbles and attached to a handle. But today they are often made from plastic or other synthetic materials.

No parranda would sound complete without the rhythmic rasping of the güiro. Güiros are also made from the long, gourdlike fruit of the *higuero* tree. As it is for the making of maracas, the fruit is hollowed out and dried. Then, into the rind of the gourd are carved long parallel indentations, which serve as sound ridges. The sound is made by drawing a forklike scraper across the ridges. The scraper is made by fixing several pieces of metal (traditionally, pieces of bicycle spokes) into a wooden handle. Like maracas, manufactured güiros are now made from a variety of materials.

somewhat like an oversized violin with a neck like that of a guitar. It originated in Spain as a four-stringed lutelike instrument. In the hands of the jíbaros in the late 1800's, six additional strings were added.

Music makers keep the beat for the parranda by using several handheld percussion instruments, especially maracas and güiros. Part of these instruments' appeal is that they can be played by

Trullas may sing carols familiar to Americans from the mainland. But more typically they sing traditional Puerto Rican carols called aguinaldos. From the Spanish word for "treat" or "little gift," aguinaldos are based on old Spanish folk songs called *décimas*. The décimas themselves

Yomo Toro, Cuatro Maestro

Puerto Ricans associate the holiday season with the sound of the cuatro. Of the several famous players the island has produced, none has achieved quite the renown of Yomo Toro, Puerto Rico's "king of the parranda." Also known as the "Jimi Hendrix of the cuatro," Toro is famous not only for his lightning-fast riffs, but for his left-handed playing. He taught himself to play upside down on a right-handed cuatro.

Victor Guillermo Toro Vega Ramos Rodríguez Acosta was born in 1934 in Guánica, a coastal village in southwestern Puerto Rico. His father and uncles, all sugar mill workers and amateur musicians, had a group called the Roosters. At age 6, he was accompanying the Roosters to their gigs.

His father was the group's cuatro player. He hung his cuatro on a wall above his bed and warned the children not to touch it. But at age 7, little Yomo began secretly teaching himself to play when his father was at work in the cane fields. One day, after he had been practicing this way for about a year, his father came home early and caught him red-handed. The little boy fell back onto the bed in fear, but his father told him to continue playing. The future virtuoso obeyed. "When I looked back at my father," Toro recalled in a 1990 *Chicago Sun Times* interview, "I saw he was crying." His father made him his first cuatro from wood he cut from a tree in the backyard.

Toro was part of a trio called "the school band." Word of his talent got around in Puerto Rican musical circles, and he was invited to join a new band called *Los Cuatro Ases de Puerto Rico,* or the Four Aces of

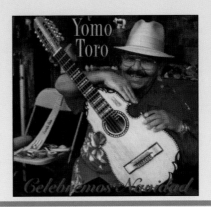

Puerto Rican cuatro virtuoso Yomo Toro released a collection of original aguinaldos called *Celebremos Navidad.*

Puerto Rico. He left for San Juan and soon was playing with some of the island's most famous musicians.

In 1953, the Four Aces performed at the Teatro Boricua in New York. Toro returned to New York with a different group of musicians to play the Teatro Puerto Rico. He moved to New York in 1956, playing with a rotating group of Latin musicians as well as popular American singers of the time.

In 1970, Toro was one of the principal musicians on salsa legend Willie Colón's Christmas album, *Asalto Navideño,* which combined traditional aguinaldos with pulsing salsa rhythms. In 1996, backed by an all-star lineup of Puerto Rican musicians and vocalists, Toro recorded a collection of his own original aguinaldos called *Celebremos Navidad.*

One of Puerto Rico's greatest cultural ambassadors for over 30 years, Toro has recorded over a dozen solo albums and has performed at Carnegie Hall and the White House.

The cuatro has become a symbol of Puerto Rican cultural identity. *Above,* a cuatro group performs in Puerto Rico. *Left,* Carmello Martell shapes the body of a cuatro in his studio in Utuado.

are a lyrical form made up of 10 couplets of 8 syllables each. The words are improvised by the singer, who engages a chorus in a lively call and response.

Aguinaldos are as varied as the holiday experience itself, embracing emotions that run the gamut from joy to melancholy, from anger to celebration, from religious ecstasy to irreverent humor. The pig who is destined to become a holiday feast, the poor reveler who threatens a flood of tears if he is not given a drink, new love accompanied by gifts of flowers during Christmastime, and the story of Christ's crucifixion are all described in popular aguinaldos.

Another kind of Christmas carol, the *villancico,* is always religious in character and related to the story of the Nativity. Villancicos have their origin in Spain and are reminders for the Christian faithful of the true meaning of the season.

The importance of the aguinaldos to the spiritual identity of the Puerto Rican people is reflected in the popular *misas de aguinaldos,* or aguinaldo Masses, celebrated at Catholic churches throughout the island at dawn on the nine days preceding Christmas Eve. At these Masses, parishioners can listen to cuatro groups play traditional Puerto Rican Christmas songs.

The Plaza de Armas in Old San Juan is colorfully decorated at Christmastime.

"Ho-ho-ho" and a bottle of rum!

Sweet, rum-flavored drinks are popular at holiday time the world over. Puerto Ricans fill their cups with a little holiday cheer in the form of coquito. Only

Puerto Rico holds the distinction of being the world's center of rum production. The Bacardí distillery in Cataño, near San Juan, is the world's largest rum distillery and, along with its museum, a popular tourist destination. The plant turns out 100,000 gallons of rum every day. Although Bacardí produces the most rum, Puerto Ricans consider Don Q their best rum. At Casa Don Q, in Old San Juan, visitors can learn about the rum company Destilería Serrallés, which has operated since 1865. Compared with Bacardí, originally a Cuban company, which moved to Puerto Rico in 1936, Destilería Serrallés is truly Puerto Rican.

To understand how Puerto Rico became the rum capital of the world, it helps to take a peek at the history of sugar production on the island. Sugar cane, a towering, bamboolike grass, is native to the islands of the South Pacific. During the 1400's, Europeans used sugar made from cane grown in North and West Africa and on nearby islands, but it was an expensive luxury item. Christopher Columbus brought sugar cane cuttings from the Canary Islands to the Caribbean in 1493. In the early 1500's, owners of large plantations naturally wanted

to focus on a crop that had the potential of bringing in large profits. They tried ginger and tobacco, among other crops, but soon discovered that sugar cane was their best bet. Not only was the island's warm, wet climate perfect for growing sugar cane, Europeans apparently were eager to buy up as much sugar as the colonists could produce. Colonists created Puerto Rico's first cane processing plant, called an *ingenio,* in 1516. In 1531, Puerto Rican cane processors sent their first shipments of refined sugar to Spain.

Making granulated sugar involves processing the sweet juice from the sugar cane to create sugar crystals. The thick, sweet, sticky liquid product that remains after this process is called molasses. The sugar processors began selling the molasses to distilleries, who used it to create another booming industry: rum.

Rum is made by adding yeast to molasses to cause fermentation, which changes the sugar into alcohol. The resulting "sugar cane wine" is then distilled to raise the alcohol content. When rum comes out of the still, it is light and clear in color and dry in flavor. This is the type of rum that people generally know as Puerto Rican rum. However, some rum producers process their rum further by aging it up to two years in oak barrels to produce a golden rum. If aging continues for another two to four years—or longer—a dark, pungent rum results.

Puerto Rican rum blends well with fruit juices to make such popular "umbrella" drinks as the piña colada and the daiquiri and, of course, with coconut milk, condensed milk, and sugar to make coquito.

Puerto Rico's African roots can be observed in a style of folk dance music called *bomba* brought to the island by West African slaves in the 1600's. It features an improvised "dialog" between dancers and drummers. The *seis bombeao* is a popular dance done at parrandas and other holiday get-togethers. The dance combines words and movement. This is how it goes: while the music is playing, a dancer will shout *"Bomba!"* The music stops and the dancer recites a funny rhyme, often one that he or she has made up on the spot. Many of these verses poke good-natured fun. Anyone or anything can be a target: family or friends, the government, celebrities, or the dancers themselves. For example:

Bomba pide el trovador, y yo le meto un bombaso,
Esta pareja mía, lo que parece es un bagazo.

Which translates, roughly,

This singer is asking for a bomba, and I'll give you a big one:
My partner looks like a chewed-up vegetable.

Revelers wear masks and dress in bright costumes at a Christmas parade in Old San Juan.

Visitors to a "Christmas Village" line up to buy souvenirs in San Juan.

The music and dancing start again, after which the partner being addressed may choose to reply with a bomba of his or her own.

Holiday season in the city

Puerto Rican cities are lovely during the holiday season. The balmy weather makes strolling and lingering outdoors a thoroughly pleasant experience. Carolers on the streets, artisans selling their holiday wares at outdoor markets, Puerto Ricans sharing a cup of coquito at a cafe, enjoying the lights and the balconies of Old San Juan— adorned with sparkling lights, pine garlands, and Christmas wreaths—all add to the holiday ambiance. In Old San Juan and other cities, life-sized Nativity scenes are displayed throughout the season, and stores show off special holiday window displays. Puerto Ricans and tourists alike take advantage of the many special holiday events and activities, such as shows presented by folkloric groups, outdoor concerts, art exhibits, and craft fairs. Children's Christmas programs are performed at the Dominican Convent; at the governor's mansion, La Fortaleza; and at City Hall.

Strolling along Old San Juan's Paseo La Princesa, or Princess Promenade, any time of year is a

Old San Juan's tree-lined pedestrian promenade Paseo La Princesa twinkles with tiny white lights at Christmastime.

charming thing. This tree-lined pedestrian promenade leads strollers along the Old City wall overlooking San Juan Bay. At Christmastime, the trees twinkle with tiny white lights, and every weekend from the beginning of December though the last weekend before Three Kings Day, visitors can enjoy theme shopping nights. Each night features a different aspect of the Puerto Rican holiday experience, and visitors can sample holiday treats and buy traditional toys and musical instruments.

> All over the island, celebrations called Encendidos de la Navidad take place.

That's not all to enjoy at the Paseo La Princesa. Starting in mid-December and continuing through January 6 is a traditional holiday show called *"Paseo de Luz,"* or "Promenade of Light." Audiences delight in the *"Teatro de Sombras,"* or "Shadows Theater," a shadow play projected on the Old City wall. Recently, the highlight of the show has been the lighting of a giant Nativity scene sculpture. Every weekend, live shows, arts and crafts exhibitions, and food stalls are featured.

Near San Cristobal, the imposing 17th-century fort at the east side of Old San Juan, the life-sized Nativity display is serenaded by carolers night and day. A similar scene can be enjoyed at Nativity scenes in the courtyard of the Siervas de María convent and of La Fortaleza.

All over the island, celebrations called *Encendidos de la Navidad* take place. The term literally means "the lighting of Christmas." The celebrations may include the turning on of Christmas lights on homes and businesses, the lighting of municipal Christmas trees, and performances. In Old San Juan, at the Paseo La Princesa, the Lighting of the Giant Christmas Tree is a traditional holiday show that features a 40-foot Christmas tree.

San Juan also hosts an outdoor holiday concert to mark its annual Encendido de la Navidad. Audiences are not deterred even when drenched by early December downpours.

White Christmas in San Juan?

Some lucky children of San Juan get to experience snow at Christmastime. Felisa Rincón de Gautier, who served as mayor of San Juan from 1946 until 1969, brought in snow by airplane to whiten children's Christmas parties. More recently, thanks to an enterprising Puerto Rican circus and figure-skating promoter named Luis Guzman, families with $30 to spare got to spend 15 minutes frolicking in imported snow.

In 2000, Guzman shipped 300 tons of snow from a small town in Quebec, Canada. It was an exercise in planning and engineering. A team of workers in Quebec used snow blowers to blast the stuff of white Christmas into freezer trucks, which hauled it to the port of New Brunswick, 1,100 miles away. The fragile cargo was packed into container ships for the 2,000-mile voyage. Meanwhile in San Juan, the "winter wonderland," a warehouse in Luís Muñoz Marín Park, was being outfitted with cooling machines backed by two generators to keep the snow frozen, and blowers to stir up simulated flurries. To prevent the graying of the snow (a condition sadly familiar to northern city dwellers), patrons were supplied with plastic booties to wear over their shoes. To top off the experience, families could accompany Santa on a helicopter ride over the city.

The island's tropical climate doesn't stop this San Juan home from putting up snowmen at Christmastime.

Nochebuena and Navidad

With all the partying that's been going on since late November, it is no wonder that many Puerto Ricans choose to spend Nochebuena (Christmas Eve) and Navidad (Christmas Day) quietly at home. This is the time when Christians in Puerto Rico celebrate the birth of Jesus Christ.

Among the opening activities of the Christmas season are the assembling of the family Nativity scene, the decorating of the tree, the hanging of lights, and the setting out of poinsettias. Families may decorate their homes with palm branches and confetti as well. The children of Puerto Rico, like their cousins on the mainland, await a visit from Santa on Christmas Eve.

For the past nine days at dawn, devout Puerto Ricans have been attending special holiday masses called misas de aguinaldos. These Masses feature cuatro bands performing aguinaldos. The parishioners might sing about the wonder of

Opposite page:
A life-sized Nativity scene is a focal point of the holiday season in Plaza Colón in Old San Juan.

Christ's birth in the traditional Puerto Rican aguinaldo "Villancico Yaucano" ("Christmas Carol from Yauco"). Yauco is a southwestern coffee-producing town in Puerto Rico; a Yaucano is a person that was born and raised in Yauco:

Ha nacido en un portal
Llenito de telarañas,
Entre la mula y el buey
El Redentor de las almas.

En Belén tocan a fuego
Del portal sale una llama;
Es una estrella del cielo
Que ha caido entre las pajas.

Translation:
He has been born in a stable
Full of spider webs
Between the mule and the ox
The Redeemer of souls.

In Bethlehem they cry fire
From the stable rises a flame;
It is a star from the sky
That has fallen in the straw.

Spanish missionaries first celebrated misas de aguinaldos in Mexico and Central America. Their purpose was to inspire the Native Americans to convert to Christianity. Wishing to offer the Indians a Christian experience that they could relate to, the missionaries modeled the morning Mass custom on an existing Indian tradition of celebrating the birth of the sun god with music and dancing. From Mexico, the misas de aguinaldos spread to Puerto Rico and throughout the Caribbean. The custom is unique to these regions and is not practiced in South America or Spain.

The misas de aguinaldos end the day before Christmas Eve and the Mass time switches to midnight, for the *misa de gallo,* or rooster Mass. The misa de gallo is so named because the rooster was supposed to have crowed at midnight on the night of Christ's birth. A verse of "Villancico Yaucano" depicts a Yaucano who brings a gift of a "qui-qui-ri-ki" (pronounced *kee kee ree KEE*) rooster, a type of small rooster, to the Christ child:

Yo soy un pobre yaucano
Que vengo de Yauco aquí
Y a mi niño Dios le traigo
Un gallo qui-qui-ri-quí.

Translation:
I am a poor Yaucano
I come from Yauco to here
And to the Baby Jesus I bring
A qui-qui-ri-qui rooster.

The holiday table

Every country has its Christmas treats, and Puerto Rico is no exception. Though the waters around the island abound with delicacies, Puerto Ricans' holiday main dishes generally abandon seafood in favor of pork, grains, plantains, and coconut. Many Puerto Rican holiday dishes began to evolve five centuries ago when resourceful Spanish nuns combined cooking styles they learned in their homeland with local techniques and ingredients, using coconut, for example, in place of milk and other ingredients that were unavailable in the new land. Today's Puerto Rican cuisine is a blend of Spanish, Taíno Indian, African, and American influences. It is known on the island as cocina criolla, or "Creole cooking."

The seasoning base of *cocina criolla* consists of two blends of herbs and spices. The first, called *adobo,* is rubbed into meat before roasting. Adobo is made with crushed peppercorns, oregano, salt, olive oil, and lime juice or vinegar. The other, *sofrito,* is the basis for many Puerto Rican soups, stews, and rice dishes. It is a blend of onions, garlic, coriander, and peppers.

On Christmas Eve, families gather for a big meal. The grand feast of the holiday season is *lechón asado,* or barbecued whole pig. To prepare it properly, a whole pig carcass is placed on a spit over a pit filled with glowing charcoal. As the pig rotates over the coals, the cook bastes it with

Lechón asado, or barbecued whole pig, is the grand feast of the holiday season. Lechoneras, restaurants that specialize in lechón asado, are very busy during the Christmas season in the district of Guavate in the city of Cayey.

A traditional Christmas meal in Puerto Rico consists of lechón asado (roasted pork), pasteles (boiled meat-filled dough rolls), arroz con gandules (rice with pigeon peas), green bananas or plantains, tembleque (coconut custard) for dessert, and coquito, a rum and coconut milk drink.

the juice of sour oranges colored with annatto. This goes on for hours until the skin is crispy brown and the meat moist and succulent. The pork is served with a sour sauce flavored with garlic, black peppercorns, chile peppers, vinegar, lime juice, and olive oil.

Green plantains roasted over hot stones are a traditional side dish, along with *arroz con gandules,* or rice with pigeon peas. Pigeon peas are legumes (plants whose seeds grow in pods). The seeds are cooked and eaten while green and tender. *Tostones,* slices of green plantain

without the facilities or desire to take on such a project need not despair. Those folks can head out to a *lechonera,* a restaurant that specializes in lechón asado. Although lechoneras operate the year around, their business booms at Christmastime, many selling as many as 35 whole roast pigs every week of Puerto Rico's long holiday season.

One of Puerto Ricans' favorite lechonera destinations near San Juan is a district called Guavate in the city of Cayey, a 30-minute drive from San Juan. The crisp evening air of this mountain locale is a most welcome Christmastime respite from the heat of the city. Hundreds of families make a trip to Guavate every weekend during the holiday season to dine on lechón and listen to Christmas music amid the gorgeous mountain scenery. Diners arriving in Guavate for a lechón feast on January 6 get an extra treat: the Children's Festival, with shows, art workshops, and handicraft demonstrations, all honoring the island's children.

Pasteles are another favorite holiday dish. Pasteles are boiled meat-filled dough rolls. The dough is made from mashed plantains or green bananas, and the filling is traditionally a combination of meat and olives.

that are fried, mashed, and fried again, are another popular side dish.

Although barbecuing a pig at home is an all-day project, often starting before dawn, the arrival of friends and family throughout the day makes it a joyful occasion. But those families

Other, recent variations may also include combinations of chickpeas and raisins. Pasteles are traditionally wrapped in banana leaves, tied with string, and then boiled. Some families gather for a pastel assembly line around Christmastime, listening to Christmas music and pitching in with the mashing, filling, wrapping, and boiling of perhaps a hundred or more pasteles for the holidays.

Topping off the holiday meal is usually *tembleque,* a coconut custard. The word tembleque is Spanish for "shaky," a perfect name for a dessert that wiggles on the plate.

Another holiday dessert is *arroz con dulce.* This rice pudding is cooked with golden raisins and coconut milk and spiced with ginger, nutmeg, cinnamon, and cloves. To make it extra fancy, it may be garnished with toasted coconut and cinnamon sticks and topped with a sauce made from chopped raisins, rum, and honey.

Cookies are popular, too. Puerto Rican favorites include shortbread cookies called *polvorones;* pastel-colored *merenguitos,* or meringues; and *besitos de coco,* or coconut cookies. Ginger crackers called *cucas* are also popular. Jellyroll cake, or *brazo gitano,* sets mouths to watering. Fruits marinated in brandy smother pound cake for the delightful *ponque.*

Puerto Ricans fill their candy dishes with *pilones,* or sugar suckers with sesame seeds; coconut cream candy called *tira y jala;* and bars made of sesame seeds and caramel, called *palitos de ajonjolí.* Special imported Spanish nougat with almonds, called *turrón,* is another treat.

Puerto Rico's first Christmas tree

Although popular wisdom relates the Puerto Rican fondness for the Christmas tree to its relationship with the United States, historians credit the introduction of the Christmas tree in Puerto Rico to a physician named Agustin Stahl. Stahl grew up in the town of Aguadilla, located along the northwest coast of the island, in the mid-1800's with his German-born father and Dutch-born mother. As a child, he listened to his father's descriptions of decorating a pine tree at Christmas. He went to Germany for his medical studies, where he experienced the custom firsthand. When he returned to

> Today's Puerto Rican cuisine is a blend of Spanish, Taíno Indian, African, and American influences.

Puerto Rico, he settled in Bayamón, on the northeast side of the island, with his family in 1865 and set up the first Christmas tree soon after. He put candles on the tree, placed glass beneath it to imitate sparkling snow and ice, and decorated it with all kinds of beautiful objects. On Christmas Eve, according to his biographer, he hung toys and treats in the tree and invited the poor children of the village to come and help themselves. The people of Bayamón christened this wonder "Dr. Stahl's Christmas Tree." Other Puerto Ricans of German descent copied Dr. Stahl's tree.

More Puerto Ricans wanted to join in the custom, but pine trees were expensive and hard to come by. Not to be daunted, they went to the mountains to cut a tree called the *sota de caballo*. People placed these trees in the rooms and on the balconies of their houses and decorated them with garlands of nuts, cotton, foil, colored paper, and bells. They also would adorn the tree with *verenjena ciroronas*, a small flower that turns from green to red after it is picked.

Nativity scenes

Puerto Ricans place Nativity scenes under the Christmas tree on Christmas Eve. Some Puerto Ricans wait until January 6, the Feast of the Epiphany, to put out the Three Kings, as this is their traditional day of arrival.

Nativity scenes are said to have been invented by Saint Francis of Assisi as a way to teach the illiterate about the birth of Christ. Spanish Franciscan missionaries introduced Nativity scenes to the New World in the late 1400's and early 1500's. Puerto Ricans began setting up Nativity scenes in their homes at Christmastime. Wealthy families would buy elaborate scenes from Europe or the United States, but families of humbler means would more likely have scenes fashioned in wood by local artisans. The simplest of these show the Baby Jesus, Mary, Joseph, and a rooster perched on a post. The rooster is important because many devout Puerto Ricans believe that the rooster crowed at the moment Christ was born. Their Christmas Eve midnight Mass is, accordingly, called the rooster Mass.

Life-sized Nativity scenes are focal points of the holiday season in San Juan, Ponce—the island's second-largest city, located along the southern coast—and other cities. In Juana Díaz, in south central Puerto Rico, a private citizen has contributed his time and effort to this very traditional

Santeros: Master Carvers of Puerto Rico

Not to be confused with Santa—though his popularity in Puerto Rico is unquestioned—a *santo* is a carved wooden figure of a saint, highly prized in Puerto Rico and throughout the Hispanic world. Santos depict the most revered Roman Catholic saints and other religious figures of Catholic legend. Santos figures were meant to be more than mere decoration. They play an important role in the spiritual life of the family. Set up along with flowers, family photos, and other treasured memorabilia to create household altars, santos become the focal point of prayers for aid and protection. Santos populate many household Nativity scenes during Christmastime. The carvers of santos, called *santeros,* hold a revered place in Puerto Rican culture.

The carving of santos was introduced to Puerto Rico in the 1500's by Spanish priests and missionaries. To convert the Taínos to Christianity, they used brightly painted figures to illustrate Biblical stories and the tales of Catholic saints. Starting sometime during the 1800's, as demand for the devotional figures grew, rural artisans taught themselves the art of santo carving. The craft centered in rural mountain villages and in the southwestern part of the island. Santeros passed their craft from one generation to the next. Generally, the figures are carved from a single block of wood.

The art of santo carving received a public relations boost in 1931. That year Dutch Dominican monks exhibited Puerto Rican santos in the Netherlands. Their efforts introduced santo figures to a wider audience.

Domingo Orta, of Ponce, is one of Puerto Rico's most famous santeros.

Domingo Orta, of Ponce, is one of Puerto Rico's most famous santeros. Orta began carving santos when he was 10 years old. One of his hand-painted 10-inch-high carvings of the Three Kings can command as much as $2,500. Pedro Pablo Rinaldi Jovet is another well-known santero from Ponce. He teaches and writes about the santeros' art in Puerto Rico, and his santos have been exhibited throughout the world. Santeros celebrate their craft during the Christmas season every year at a festival in Orocovis, in the heart of Puerto Rico.

way of acknowledging the season. Enrique Marrero has created a scale model not only of the manger, but of the surrounding countryside, with bodies of water, streets and buildings, churches, bridges, and shepherds. "The Nativity of Juana Díaz," as it's known, is made to scale and stretches more than 40 feet. Marrero made all the elements by hand little by little over the years for his private satisfaction. But now every year at Christmastime he opens it to the public.

Children pose with a rooster and hen during a Christmas gathering in the mountains of Lares. Many devout Puerto Ricans believe that a rooster crowed at the moment Christ was born. Christmas Eve midnight Mass is called the rooster Mass.

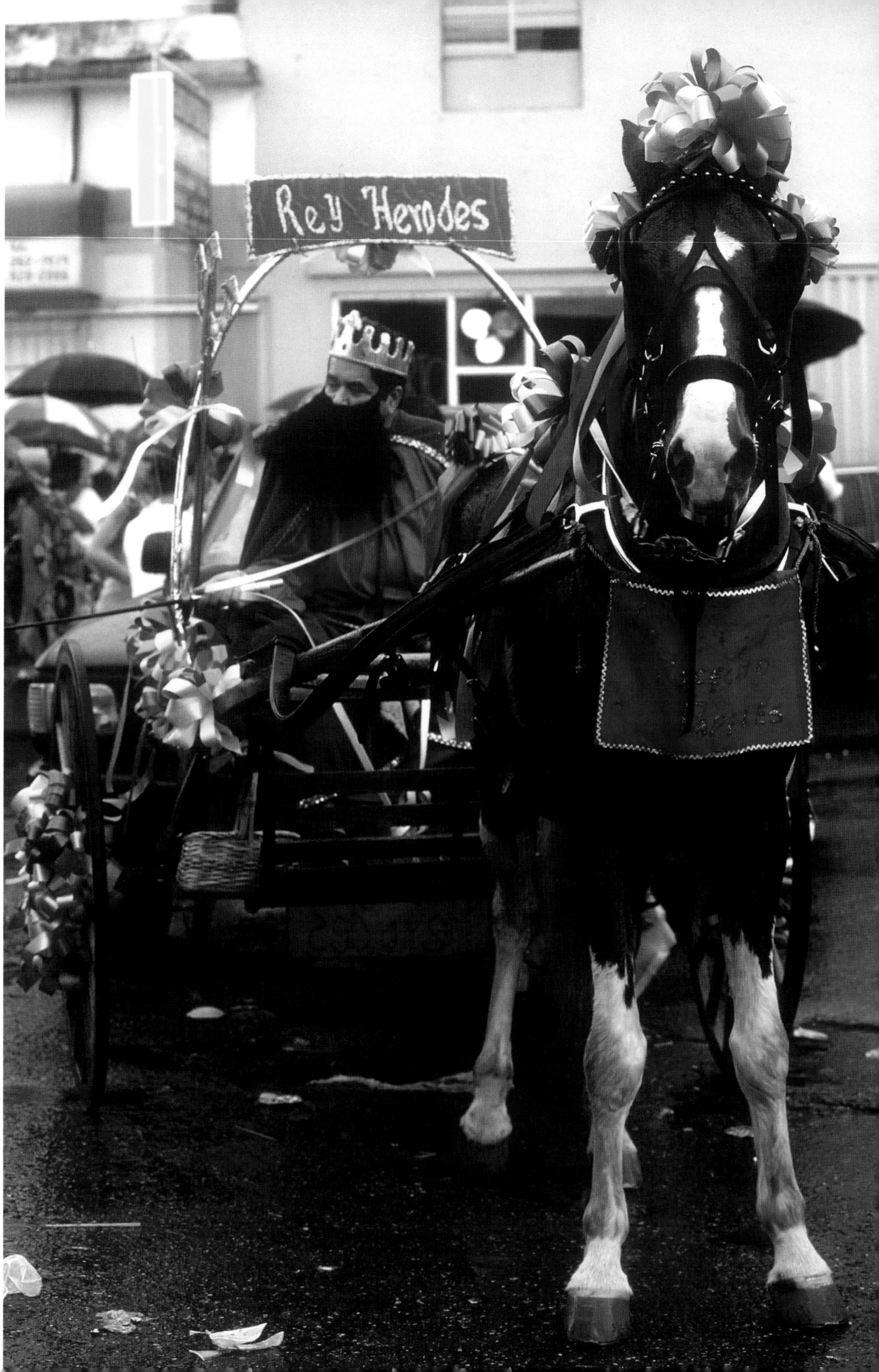
Rey Herodes

Other Holiday Season Festivals

With the autumn rainy season at an end and the dazzling sunshine, blue skies, and warm breezes of December making outdoor activities so pleasant, it's no wonder that the holiday season has such a wide array of cultural fairs and festivals. During December and January, Puerto Ricans have many opportunities to express their love of celebration—and their "Puertoricanness"—during the holiday season. These truly unique folk festivals include the Petate Festival and the Festival de las Máscaras, or Festival of the Masks.

Festival of the Masks

The Day of the Innocents is celebrated every December 28 to commemorate a ghastly Biblical story. After Jesus's birth, the Roman king Herod, hearing the news that a great Jewish leader had been born in fulfillment of the prophecies, feared that his throne might be challenged. To stave off an end to his rule, he ordered the slaying of all boys in Bethlehem under the age of 2 years. Herod's soldiers carried out the order to the horror of the people. But Jesus and his family escaped by fleeing to Egypt.

Although the original story is full of tragedy, it has resulted in one of Puerto Rico's most colorful—and rowdy—folk festivals, Festival de las Máscaras, which takes place every year on the two

Opposite page:
On December 28th, the village of Hatillo celebrates the Day of the Innocents with the Festival of the Masks. This festival honors the memory of the innocent children who were killed by King Herod when he tried to destroy the Christ child.

days after Christmas in Hatillo, a village in the dairy farming region on the island's northern coast.

The festival includes costumed "troublemakers," referred to as *máscaras,* who pile 10 or 15 strong on colorful "floats" to descend upon the city streets. These floats, called *carrozas,* are actually fantastically decorated automobiles, often jeeps, that have been specially outfitted with high-powered sirens, deafening public-address systems, and souped-up suspension systems. The purpose of all this customizing is to allow the máscaras to make as much ruckus as possible. As they roam the city streets, they blow their sirens and yell and holler through their PA systems. They may leap from their floats to playfully harass onlookers, who may be doused with water, squirted with shaving cream or maple syrup, or scared with rubber snakes. Young men may try to kidnap pretty girls and spirit them away on their floats. They even stop at people's houses to play pranks.

But the dramatic automotive displays are perhaps the most exciting part of the celebration. The floats' special suspension systems allow the máscaras to raise the front end to a steep angle. They will often do this while barreling down the street at a fairly high speed. The máscaras also rock their floats back and forth. Spectators hold their breath as they wait for the floats to tip over and spill their masked cargo onto the street. But the sturdy floats keep their rubber on the road (perhaps thanks to the prayers that the máscaras traditionally recite before setting out) and the revelry continues. All paths lead to the main square of Hatillo, where awards are given for the best costumes and floats at the end of the celebration.

The máscaras' masks are made of molded colored wire mesh and sometimes decorated with paint. Their elaborate costumes are custom-made and often cost hundreds of dollars. Each group dresses in identical costumes. Many are based on a Puerto Rican theme, such as the Puerto Rican flag or the little tree frog known as the coquí. To allow the máscaras to stay relatively cool during their day-long exertions in the hot December sun, costumes are made of cotton. Cotton also holds up well to the periodic hosing down that máscaras use to beat the heat. Costumes are festooned with *cascabeles,* or jingle bells. The jingle bells not only make a festive sound, but provide lots of fun for the children, who love to collect fallen

The máscaras' elaborate costumes are custom-made and often cost hundreds of dollars. Each group dresses in identical costumes.

bells from the street. The bravest children—perhaps future máscaras themselves—like to torment the máscaras by sneaking up on them to pluck a jingle bell from their costumes.

The Hatillo festival is said to have started during the 1800's, at the time the town was founded. Hatillo's original inhabitants, from the Canary Islands, brought their tradition of pre-Lenten masked revelry with them. The Canary Islanders' tradition involved men dressing as women and visiting the homes of friends and relatives to dance, tease, and beg for pocket change. It was not related in any way to the Day of the Innocents.

At the end of the 1800's and in the early 1900's, the tradition underwent further evolution. Men no longer dressed as women, and their costumes became more elaborate. Now they traveled from house to house in groups, rather than singly, and their antics became more rowdy. Máscaras on horseback dressed as Herod's evil soldiers sometimes "kidnapped"

Máscaras in colorful carrozas (decorated automobiles)
descend upon the streets of Hatillo during the village's
Festival de las Máscaras.

the children of their friends and relatives. Since only children who were outdoors on December 28 were taken, children were often told to stay home that day. The unfortunate youngsters who didn't remain indoors were spirited off to a distant secret location. Their parents sometimes had to search for them for days. Once they found them, they had to ransom them with gifts for the "soldiers." But once the children returned home, they were welcomed with much celebrating. Even in more innocent times, needless to say, this practice was quite frightening for children and parents alike, and it's no surprise that it was abandoned.

Hatillo residents wanted to retain their máscaras tradition, but also wanted to do away with the "antisocial" elements that had crept in and create a celebration unique to the town of Hatillo that would entertain townsfolk, other Puerto Ricans, and tourists alike.

So during the 1950's, town officials moved the festival to December 28 and organized it as a municipal parade, complete with judging and prizes. Today the festival may attract more than 100 floats and include close to 3,000 máscaras. The town also holds a Children's Masks Festival—*Festival del Niño—Día de Inocentes*—on December 27, with activities just for kids.

The town of Moca, in the northwest corner of the island, has a similar celebration on December 28, but it differs in character. The men of the town dress as the good soldiers who announced that the infant Jesus had survived the slaughter. They dress in frilly, sequined costumes and wear hats adorned with Christmas bows. Ten groups of costumed dancers and musicians, each representing a different neighborhood in Moca, join in a parade down one of the town's main streets.

Petate Festival

In the town of Sabana Grande in the southwestern part of the island, a festival celebrating the *petate* is held every December a week or two before Christmas.

A petate is a sleeping mat woven from the fronds of the brittle thatch, or broom, palm.

The craft originated in pre-Columbian times among the Taíno Indians and flourished in the 1800's and the first decades of the 1900's. New tender palm fronds are picked and then dried for several days. Artisans weave the dry fronds into long strips called *pleitas,* which are about 8 inches wide and more than 25 feet long. Using a large wooden needle, the pleitas are sewn together to make a petate. Working people of modest means traditionally used petates as sleeping mats. They were placed on the floor at night and hung up in the corner of the room during the day. Today, petates and other crafts made of woven palm fronds decorate the homes of many Puerto Ricans.

Sabana Grande is known as the Town of the Petateros, or petate-makers, because it is the center of the practice of this disappearing skill. The festival, which originated in 1979, was started not only to preserve the tradition of petate weaving, but also to tie it in with the Christmas celebration. The festival consists of three days of petate crafts demonstrations, food, and music. More than 50 artisans demonstrate how to weave palm fronds. A parade combines elements of the holiday season—such as Christmas- and

Three Kings-themed floats—with Puerto Rican culture and local flavor. School bands play, drill-teams march, dancers perform, masked revelers frolic, and children and adults don pavas and traditional costumes.

Other fairs of the holiday season

As if Hatillo hasn't had enough partying with its Day of the Innocents Festival, at the same time it also holds the *Festival del Güiro y Música Típica,* the Festival of the Güiro and Typical

Puerto Rican tradition says that for the rest of the year to come the home will remain in whatever condition it is in as the old year ends. Naturally, everyone wants their surroundings in tip-top shape.

Music, a festival to honor the güiro, the beloved accompaniment to Puerto Rican Christmas music. Not to be outdone, the town of Las Piedras, on the eastern edge of the island, holds a 10-day güiro festival the first week of January.

The largest art fair in Puerto Rico, the Bacardí Artisans' Fair, takes place on the first two Sundays of December on the grounds of the Bacardí rum distillery, in Cataño. Besides displays of ceramics, masks, jewelry, holiday crafts, and woodcarvings by more than 100 Puerto Rican artists, the fair includes rides, traditional Puerto Rican treats, music, and a traditional troubadour contest.

The troubador contest, something like a poetry slam, honors the best practitioners of the ancient Spanish art of the décima, the poetry form that is the basis for the typical Puerto Rican Christmas carols called aguinaldos. Décimas consist of 10 lines of 8 syllables each, with a complex rhyme scheme. Contestants are given one line of a chorus and provided with musical accompaniment (a cuatro, guitar, and güiro) and must create a décima on the spot. The musicians start playing and the poets start reciting. Judges award prizes based not only on strict adherence to rhyme schemes and rhythms of the décima form, but also on creativity, meaning, and speed of execution.

Mid-December also sees the annual celebration of that mainstay of Puerto Rican holiday cuisine—the gandúl, or pigeon pea—at *El Festival del Gandúl,* in the central Puerto Rican town of Villalba. Gandúl season peaks in December, which no doubt contributes to gandules' cherished place on the holiday menu. At the carnival a huge pot of *asopao de gandules* (pigeon pea soup) is prepared—enough to feed 6,000 merrymakers.

Año Viejo

In Puerto Rico, New Year's Eve is called *Año Viejo,* or Old Year, because it is the night when everyone says farewell to the year gone by. As in many other countries of the world, the evening is celebrated with parties and revelry. But New Year's Eve day is spent in a frenzy of cleaning—the house, the yard, the car, even the streets. Puerto Rican tradition says that for the rest of the year to come the home will remain in whatever condition it is in as the old year ends. Naturally, everyone wants their surroundings in tip-top shape.

Typically, friends gather for feasting and merrymaking that lead up to the hour of midnight. As the clock chimes, Puerto Ricans eat 12 grapes one by one, for good luck in each of the 12 months to come. At the moment the new year arrives, everyone yells *"Feliz Año Nuevo"* ("Happy New Year"), car horns blare, fireworks blaze, and hugs and kisses are exchanged. Many people also throw a pail of water out a window or off a balcony to symbolically separate themselves from the mistakes of the past year and burn incense to further purify the home. Dancing, music, and feasting may continue well into the night.

No New Year's Eve celebration would be complete without the reciting of the poem called "El Brindis del Bohemio," or "The Toast of the Bohemian," written in 1941 by the Mexican poet Guillermo Aguirre y Fierro in El Paso, Texas. A New Year's Eve tradition similar to the singing of "Auld Lang Syne," many Puerto Ricans tune their radios to stations that air professional recitations of this beloved poem. The poem tells of a group of friends who toast the New Year as they relate lighthearted anecdotes of their experiences during the previous year. The last drinker, however, offers his toast to the memory of his dead mother, bringing a melancholy end to their merrymaking.

El Brindis del Bohemio

De Guillermo Aguirre Fierro [excerta]

En torno de una mesa de cantina,
en una noche de invierno,
rogocijadamente departían
seis alegres bohemios.

Los ecos de sus risas escapaban
y de aquel barrio quieto
iban a interrumpir el imponente
y profundo silencio.

El humo de olorosos cigarrillos
en espirales se elevaba al cielo,
simbolizando al revolverse en nada,
la vida de los sueños.

Pero en todos los labios había risas,
inspiración en todos los cerebros,
y, repartidas en la mesa, copas
pletóricas de ron, whisky o ajenjo.

Era curioso ver aquel conjunto,
aquel grupo bohemio,
del que brotaba la palabra chusca,
la que vierte veneno,
lo mismo que, melosa y delicada,
la música de un verso.

A cada nueva libación, las penas
hallábanse más lejos
del grupo, y nueva inspiración llegaba
a todos los cerebros,
con el idilio roto que venía
en alas del recuerdo.

Olvidaba decir que aquella noche,
aquel grupo bohemio
celebraba entre risas, libaciones,
chascarrillos y versos,
la agonía de un año que amarguras
dejó en todos los pechos,
y la llegada, consecuencia lógica,
del "feliz año nuevo."

Una voz varonil dijo de pronto:
"Las doce compañeros;
Digamos el 'requiéscat' por el año
que ha pasado a formar entre los muertos.
¡Brindemos por el año que comienza!
porque nos traiga ensueños,
porque no sea su equipaje un cúmulo
de amargos desconsuelos."

"Brindo," dijo otra voz, "por la esperanza
que a la vida nos lanza,
de vencer los rigores del destino;
por la esperanza, nuestra dulce amiga,
que las penas mitiga
y convierte en vergel nuestro camino."

. . . .

"¡Bravo!"dijeron todos, "inspirado
esta noche has estado
y hablaste bueno, breve y substancioso.
El turno es de Raúl, alce su copa
y brinde por ... Europa,
ya que su extranjerismo es delicioso."

"Bebo y brindo," clamó el interpelado;
"brindo por mi pasado,
que fue de luz, de amor y de alegría,
y en el que hubo mujeres seductoras
y frentes soñadoras
que se juntaron con la frente mía."

. . . .

"Yo brindo," dijo Juan, "porque en mi mente
brote un torrente
de inspiración divina y seductora;
porque vibre en las cuerdas de mi lira
el verso que suspira,
que sonríe, que canta y que enamora."

. . . .

Siguió la tempestad de frases vanas,
de aquellas tan humanas
que hallan en todas partes acomodo,
y en cada frase de entusiasmo ardiente,
hubo ovación creciente,
y libaciones, y reír y todo.

. . . .

Sólo faltaba un brindis, el de Arturo,
el del bohemio puro,
de noble corazón y gran cabeza;
aquel que sin ambages declaraba
que sólo ambicionaba
robarle inspiración a la tristeza.

. . . .

"Brindo por la mujer, mas no por esa
en la que halláis consuelo en la tristeza,
rescoldo del placer ¡desventurados!
no por ésa que os brinda sus hechizos
cuando besáis sus rizos
artificiosamente perfumados.

"Yo no brindo por ella, compañeros,
siento por esta vez no complaceros.
Brindo por la mujer, pero por una,
por la que me brindó sus embelesos
y me envolvió en sus besos,
por la mujer que me arrulló en la cuna.

"Por la mujer que me enseñó de niño
lo que vale el cariño
exquisito, profundo y verdadero;
por la mujer que me arrulló en sus brazos
y que me dio en pedazos,
uno por uno su corazón entero.

"¡Por mi madre! bohemios, por la anciana
que piensa en el mañana
como en algo muy dulce y muy deseado,
porque sueña tal vez, que mi destino
me señala el camino
por el que volveré pronto a su lado.

. . . .

"Por la anciana infeliz que sufre y llora
y que del cielo implora
que vuelva yo muy pronto a estar con ella;
por mi madre, bohemios, que es dulzura
vertida en amargura
y en esta noche de mi vida, estrella."

El bohemio calló; ningún acento
profanó el sentimiento
nacido del dolor y la ternura:
y pareció que sobre aquel ambiente
flotaba inmensamente
un poema de amor y de amargura.

The Toast of the Bohemian

By Guillermo Aguirre Fierro [excerpt]

Around a table in a bar,
on a winter night,
six happy bohemians
were joyfully conversing.

The echoes of their laughter escaped
and went to interrupt the imposing
and profound silence
of that quiet neighborhood.

The smoke of fragrant cigarettes
rose in spirals to the sky,
symbolizing while revolving in nothingness,
the life of dreams.

But there were smiles on all the lips,
inspiration in all the minds,
and, spread out on the table, glasses
brimming with rum, whiskey, or absinthe.

It was curious to see that group,
that bohemian group,
from which the comical word gushed forth,
the one that pours poison,
the same as, sweet and delicate,
the music of verse.

With each new libation, sorrows
found themselves farther away
from the group, and new inspiration came
to all the minds,
with the broken idyll that came
on the wings of memory.

I forgot to say that that night,
that bohemian group
celebrated amid laughter, libations,
jokes and verses,
the dying of a year that left
sorrows in all their hearts,
and the advent, logical consequence,
of the "happy new year."

A manly voice suddenly said:
"It's midnight, friends;
Let's say the 'resquiescat' for the year
that has passed to abide among the dead.
Let's toast for the year that begins!
for it to bring us dreams,
for its baggage not be a pile
of bitter despair."

"I toast," said another voice, "for the hope
that impels us to live,
to defeat the rigors of destiny;
for hope, our sweet friend,
that mitigates the sorrows
and turns our path into a garden."

. . . .

"Bravo!" cried all, "inspired
you have been tonight
and your talk was good, brief and solid.
It is Raul's turn, raise your glass
and toast for ... Europe,
because its foreignness is delicious."

"I drink and toast," exclaimed the listener;
"I toast for my past
that was of light, of love and of joy,
and in which there were seductive women
and dreaming brows
that drew close to this brow of mine."

. . . .

"I toast," said Juan, "so that in my mind
there may spring up a torrent
of divine and seductive inspiration;
that the strings of my lyre may vibrate with
the verse that sighs,
that smiles, that sings and that charms."

. . . .

The tempest of vain phrases continued,
of those so human
that find acceptance everywhere,
and to each phrase of ardent enthusiasm,
there was increasing ovation,
and libation, and laughter and everything.

. . . .

There was only one toast remaining, Arturo's,
that of the pure bohemian,
of noble heart and great mind;
the one who frankly declared
that he only sought
to steal inspiration from sadness.

. . . .

"I toast for the woman, but not the one
in whom you find solace for your grief,
embers of pleasure, unfortunates!
Not for that one that offers you her enchantments
when you kiss her curls,
artificially perfumed.

"I do not toast for her, my friends,
I'm sorry about not pleasing you this time.
I toast for a woman, but for one,
for the one who gave me her delights
and wrapped me in her kisses,
for the woman who lulled me in the cradle.

"For the woman who taught me as a child
the worth of affectionate love,
exquisite, profound and truthful;
for the woman who lulled me in her arms
and who gave me in pieces,
one by one, her entire heart.

"For my mother! Bohemians, for the old woman
who thinks about tomorrow
as of something very sweet and much desired,
because she dreams perhaps, that my fate
shows me the way
by which I will soon return to her side.

. . . .

"For the unhappy old woman who suffers and weeps
and who implores heaven
that to be with her I soon return;
for my mother, bohemians, who is sweetness
poured into bitterness
and in this night of my life, a star."

The bohemian fell silent; no word
profaned the sentiment
born from pain and tenderness:
and it seemed that over that gathering
floated immensely,
a poem of love and bitterness.

The Coming of the Kings

The Three Kings who followed the Star of Bethlehem to present the infant Jesus with gifts, as depicted in the New Testament, are much revered in Spanish-speaking countries. The legendary date of their arrival, January 6, or the Feast of the Epiphany, is celebrated in Puerto Rico as Día de los Tres Reyes, or Three Kings Day.

Three Kings Day is as big, or bigger, than Christmas in Puerto Rico. Stores, businesses, and government offices are closed. Families gather for feasting and merrymaking, and gifts are exchanged. But most of all, many people say, Three Kings Day is for children.

Like many of their Christmas traditions, Puerto Ricans have the Spanish to thank for their rich traditions of celebrating Three Kings Day. Countless crafts and carols and much pageantry surround the celebration of Three Kings Day in Puerto Rico.

On Three Kings Eve, the city streets bustle with excitement. In Ponce, the traffic snarls to gridlock as citizens rush about to make last-minute purchases at the market stalls under the twinkling lights in the Plaza of Delights. In Old San Juan, families sleep out on the sidewalks outside La Fortaleza, the 500-year-old governor's mansion, to make sure they'll be among the first to receive the gifts distributed by the governor the next day. The party goes on all day, with music and entertainment for kids.

Families gather for still more parties. In many households,

Opposite page:
This wood carving of the Three Kings is displayed at the Bacardí Artisans' Fair, in Cataño. This largest fair in Puerto Rico takes place on the first two Sundays of December on the grounds of the Bacardí rum distillery.

Sila María Calderón, *center,* Puerto Rico's first woman governor, opens the gate of the Puerto Rico governor's mansion to give Three Kings Day presents to thousands of children who came with their parents.

Three Kings celebrations are more festive and boisterous than Christmas Eve celebrations. People drink coquito and feast on pasteles, tembleque, and arroz con gandules. They sing and dance well into the night. At Three Kings Eve Masses throughout the island, priests offer effigies of the Baby Jesus for the faithful to kiss.

All Puerto Rican children know that, just as Santa does on Christmas Eve, on the night of January 5 the Three Kings make their rounds, passing out gifts to the well-behaved. Children prepare for the kings' arrival by filling a shoe box with grass and putting it, along with a dish of water, under their beds. Their list of gift wishes might be included

everything according to tradition and been well-behaved little *niños* all year (and maybe even if they haven't), the relatives will cheerfully arrive at their house on January 6. The boxes under their arms will be emptied of grass and filled with toys and treats for the children.

The story of the Three Kings

According to gospel stories, at the hour of Christ's birth, a previously unseen star blazed in the heavens. Among the many people who noted this unusual astronomical phenomenon were three "priest-kings" from the east—known today as the Magi, the Three Wise Men, or, simply, the Three Kings. These rulers, well versed in the language of prophecy, knew that a "king of kings" had been born. Thus, they set out to pay their respects, using the star as their navigational aid to find the newborn.

Religious scholarship provides conflicting information about the identities of the Three Kings and the details of their visit. Popular tradition, based on medieval accounts, accurate or not, fills in the blanks. The Three Kings are identified as Gaspar, Melchior, and Balthazar. Middle-aged, dark-skinned Balthazar, the king of

for good measure. Unlike cookies and milk, which are meant to refresh Santa during his tiring journey, the grass and water are a gift for the kings' camels. Children also make sure a box of grass and water goes under the bed of every grandparent, aunt and uncle, godparent, and other person who might be good for a little gift. If they've done

Camels, representing the tradition of the Three Kings, eat grass in San Juan. Children prepare for the kings' arrival by placing grass and water under their own beds as gifts for the kings' camels.

Ethiopia, offered the fragrant tree bark extract called frankincense. This substance was burned during religious services, and the gift acknowledged Christ as a high priest. Balthazar's feast day is January 6. Melchior, the oldest of the kings, with a long gray beard, was king of Arabia. His gift of gold proclaimed Christ as king. His feast day is January 7. Gaspar, king of Tarsus, was a young man in his 20s. His gift—myrrh, a precious bark extract that was used in embalming, in medicine, and in perfume—symbolized Christ as a healer. Gaspar's feast day is January 8.

When the kings arrived at the manger, they threw themselves face down in worship before the Holy Family, presented the infant Jesus with their gifts of gold, frankincense, and myrrh, and offered predictions for his future. When they left, it is said, angels of the Lord led them home by a route along which they were able to find food and water for their weary camels.

The Puerto Ricans have a traditional aguinaldo called "De Tierra Lejana Venimos," or "From a Distant Home" ("Song of the Wise Men"), celebrating the Three Kings:

De tierra lejana, Venimos a verte,
Nos sirve de guia, La Estrella de
*   Oriente.*

Estribillo:
O brillante estrella que anuncias la
*   aurora,*
No nos falte nunca tu luz bienhechora,
Gloria en las alturas al Hijo de Dios,
Gloria en las alturas y en la tierra amor.

Al recien nacido que es Rey de los
*   reyes,*
Oro le regalo para ornar sus sienes.

Estribillo

Como es Dios el Niño le regalo
*   incienso,*
Perfume con alma que sube hasta
*   el cielo.*

Estribillo

Al Niño del cielo que bajó a la tierra,
Le regalo mirra que inspira tristeza.

Estribillo

Translation:
From a distant home, The Savior we
*   come seeking,*
Using as our guide the star, so brightly
*   beaming.*

Refrain:
Lovely Eastern Star, that tells us of
*   God's morning,*
Heaven's wondrous light,

O never cease Thy shining, peace and
*   love to men.*
Glory in the Highest to the Son
*   of Heaven,*
And upon the earth be peace and love to
*   all*

Glowing gold I bring to the new-born
*   Babe so holy,*
Token of His pow'r to reign above
*   in glory.*

Refrain

Frankincense I bring to the Child of
*   God's own choosing,*
Token of our pray'rs to Heaven
*   ever rising.*

Refrain

Bitter myrrh I bring to give the
*   infant Jesus,*
Token of the pain that He will bear
*   to save us.*

Refrain

Three Kings in wood

Among the most popular santos, or carved saint figures, in Puerto Rico are the Three Kings. Devout Puerto Ricans consider the Three Kings powerful miracle workers. During the three months before Three Kings Day, they pray to the Three Kings for blessings in return for special honors. If their prayers are fulfilled, they give thanks to the

Traditional wood figures, called santos, are carved by craftworkers known as santeros. Most santos represent a saint or a religious scene.

kings on Three Kings Day by means of such devotions as building special altars or setting off fireworks. In Puerto Rico, Three Kings Day is often commemorated by ceremonies called *velorios de reyes,* in which believers pray around an altar that features santos figures of the Three Kings.

Puerto Rican tradition has altered the portrayal of the Three Kings according to the islands' own ethnic heritage and folkways. In European tradition, the kings are shown riding camels through the desert, while traditional Puerto Rican images of the Three Kings show them on horseback. Two kinds of Three Kings figures are familiar to Puerto Ricans. One type, meant to serve as an object of devotion, shows the Three Kings facing the viewer. The other type, meant to serve a storytelling purpose, shows the Three Kings in profile gazing up at the Star of Bethlehem.

The kings are usually portrayed as one unit attached to a flat base. They are dressed in flowing robes and wear crowns. In the Spanish Caribbean tradition, Melchior, as in European tradition, is the central figure. He is the dark-skinned king. He rides a light-colored horse and carries a scepter. The other two kings are light-skinned. Balthazar rides a black horse and Gaspar a brown one. All three carry boxes, representing their gifts of gold, frankincense, and myrrh.

The Three Kings are also sometimes depicted accompanied by the "Three Marías." According to legend, these beautiful young women were invited by the kings to Bethlehem to worship the Child. When the travelers arrived, the Virgin Mary made the night last an hour longer so that the damsels would not be home late.

Three Kings Day celebrations

Three Kings Day celebrations take place throughout the island. The *Fiesta de Reyes Isabelinos,* in the town of Isabela, located along the island's northwest coast, preserves the Three Kings tradition with a parade of Christmas floats and an appearance by the Three Kings themselves. Even the El Comandante Horse Race Track, in Canóvanas, located in the northwest corner of the island, gets into the holiday spirit, with its Three Kings Day Classic thoroughbred race. Arecibo, a coastal town in north central Puerto Rico, celebrated Three Kings Day recently by presenting the citizens with the "world's largest pastel," a 300-pound boiled meat-and-dough culinary marvel. No sooner had the townsfolk dabbed the last of its crumbs from their chins than the town began planning for the unveiling of even bigger pasteles for future celebrations.

Three Kings Day in Juana Díaz

The most elaborate and oldest Three Kings Day celebration

The Three Kings, Gaspar, *left,* Melchior, *center,* and Balthazar, *right,* arrive in Caguas to meet with underprivileged children in honor of Three Kings Day.

A home in San Juan shows its patriotic spirit at Christmastime with this nativity scene that includes the Three Kings sailing in the Santa María.

takes place in Juana Díaz, a medium-sized town in central Puerto Rico, about 10 miles from the southern coast.

Here, the tradition of Three Kings Day is kept with an energy and intensity that few religious celebrations can exceed. Hundreds of men, women, boys, and girls dressed as shepherds and shepherdesses turn out to join in an elaborate reenactment of the Biblical story of the Three Kings' visit to the newborn Savior.

The festivities begin on Three Kings Eve, January 5, with activities for children, clowns, a Mass, and a concert. The next morning, around 10 a.m., the story of the visit of the Three Kings to the newborn Jesus is reenacted.

The parade is led by hundreds of townspeople dressed as shepherds and shepherdesses. The first to set off from Barbosa Street are shepherds and shepherdesses carrying the flags of many countries. Their costumes are colorful; some are typical traditional Spanish folk costumes: wide, ruffled skirts and a matching vest adorned with sequins, white blouses, and a kerchief for the head for the shepherdesses. For the shepherds, black pants, a white shirt, a vest, and a Spanish hat. Others dress as the "Arab shepherds," in turbans and robes of white and pastel pink, purple, beige, blue, or green.

Bringing up the rear are three men of the town, richly costumed as the Three Kings. As the procession wends its way through the town, everyone joins in the singing of "La Marcha de

The National Caravan

When sculptor Naldo de la Loma finished his Monument of the Three Kings, he insisted on transporting it to Juana Díaz, not by a safe route, but straight through the Cordillera Central, which he considered the heart and soul of Puerto Rico. In addition, he wanted the sculpture to make a special stop in his hometown of Barranquitas, in central Puerto Rico. Juana Díaz event officials objected, fearing that the chances for damage were too great. But de la Loma insisted, and the sculpture wended its way to Juana Díaz via the mountain towns of Bayamón, Naranjito, Comerío, Barranquitas, Aibonito, Coamo, and Villalba.

The monument's journey received much attention from the people as well as the Puerto Rican media. As the monument passed through the town of Barranquitas, hundreds of people greeted it with flowers and Puerto Rican music. When it arrived in Juana Díaz, much earlier than scheduled, the surprised townspeople spontaneously turned out in the town square to greet it.

Organizers of the Juana Díaz event considered this response to the sculpture an indication of the significance of their yearly tradition. In order to celebrate their cultural traditions and remind Puerto Ricans of the spiritual basis of the Three Kings celebration, they decided to stage a similar pilgrimage the following year. The second National Caravan of the Three Kings visited towns throughout

Each of the kings in Naldo de la Loma's Monument of the Three Kings in Juana Díaz represents one of the three main aspects of Puerto Rican ethnic heritage: Indian, African, and Spanish.

Puerto Rico. Since the year of its inauguration in 1985, the caravan has visited nearly every Puerto Rican town, in addition to New York and the Dominican Republic.

Three boys portray the Three Kings at a Three Kings Day parade in Old San Juan. Three Kings Day honors the Three Wise Men who brought gifts to the Baby Jesus.

los Reyes" ("The Three Kings' March"):

En pos de la estrella
los Reyes presurosos
caminan del Oriente
al portal de Belén,
de Belén.

Venid, venid mortales
y los pastores también.
Adoremos todos
al Dios de Israel.

Translation:

In pursuit of a star,
The Kings hastened from the
  Orient
to the manger in Bethlehem,
in Bethlehem.

Come, come mortals
and shepherds, too.
Let us all adore
the King of Israel.

After a 45-minute procession, there is the Proclamation of the Prophecies, in which the Three Kings convey their predictions for Christ's time on Earth. Then the Dialog of the Kings and Shepherds is recited, in which the kings explain the miracle that has occurred—that God has been born in human form—and explain the meaning of the gifts they bear. Then a Mass is celebrated in the town square.

The kings then proceed to the manger, where the Holy Family awaits. The kings present the Baby Jesus, played by a real live baby boy, with their gifts and bow down before him in adoration. The pageant ends with the kings holding up the boy to present him to the crowd.

This is all finished by about 1 o'clock, and the rest of the day and much of the night is given over to entertainment, artisans exhibiting their crafts, food and drink, and music and celebration.

The origin of the celebration

The town of Juana Díaz has been staging its Three Kings Day pageant since 1884. At that time, a parish priest by the name of Father Valentín Echevarría decided that it would benefit his parishioners to reenact the story of the Three Kings. The tradition of staging dramatic reenactments of Bible stories dates back to the Middle Ages, but it was largely abandoned during the Renaissance. Still, Father Echevarría was acquainted with the tradition, and so he presented the idea to the townspeople.

The first parade of kings and shepherds took place on the road between Juana Díaz and Coamo. The participants dressed in costumes typical of the Spanish provinces of Castile and Aragon and were accompanied by musicians. After the presentation of gifts, a Mass in the church, the adoration, and a closing ceremony, the kings visited the homes of the townspeople.

The event was a hit, and was carried out every year. The tradition took the form it has today with the arrival of a new parish priest, Father Ramiro García Rey, in 1940. He felt that much of the spirit had gone out of the Three Kings celebration, so to inject new life into the proceedings, he decided to add the dialog between the kings and shepherds. He is given credit for transforming the tradition into the renowned event it has become today.

The Monument of the Three Kings

Since 1985, Juana Díaz town square has had a much beloved statue of the Three Kings. The sculptor, Naldo de la Loma, worked on the monument at the Institute of Puerto Rican Culture, in San Juan, with the help of many assistants, among them young people of Juana Díaz, who traveled to the capital to volunteer their time and effort. De la Loma received no money for his work, which he dedicated as a gift to the children of the world.

De la Loma designed the monument to be rich in symbolic detail. The kings, shown in a tight grouping and facing one another, each represent one of the three main aspects of Puerto Rican ethnic heritage. One has Indian features and clothing and offers the Baby Jesus a figure of an Indian god, as if to say, "I give up my old religion and now worship only you." The second king, with African features, offers a drum, symbolizing that, like music, Christ is a source of joy. The third, bearded and with European features meant to suggest Puerto Rican's Spanish heritage, kneels with a Bible in hand. The artist wanted to acknowledge that it was the Spanish people who brought the word of Christ and the message of salvation to the island.

At first, the monument was installed in the town square without a pedestal. But de la Loma's vision was for the Three Kings procession to enter the Juana Díaz town square through an arched pedestal under the monument. The artist and the town had to wait 11 years for it, but his dream came true when just such a pedestal was completed as part of the renovation of the town square in 1996.

Octavas and Octavitas

For most of Puerto Rico, Three Kings Day marks the official end of the holiday season. But Puerto Ricans have an opportunity to extend the holiday even further if they wish. According to custom, anyone who receives a visit on Three Kings Day is supposed to pay a visit in return eight days later.

Las Octavas, or "the eights," traditionally began on January 9, the day after the last of the Three Kings' feast days. It consisted of eight days of giving praise to the Three Kings and commemorating the period during which the adoration of the Baby Jesus took place. Devout Puerto Ricans may say special rosaries during this time. *Las Octavitas* means "the little eights," and were eight additional days of devotion immediately following las Octavas.

During this interlude, a traditional celebration called Bethlehem Day may occur on January 12. On this day, groups of children may parade through town. Leading the procession are three children robed as the Three Kings, followed by more children dressed as angels, shepherds, and flute players, all carrying flower garlands.

In actual practice today, many Puerto Ricans use January 16 to take down the lights, put the pavas back into storage, drag the tree out to the alley, and say good-by to another holiday season. No doubt there are Boricuans who are already looking forward to next Christmas season.

CRAFTS

Coquí Ornament

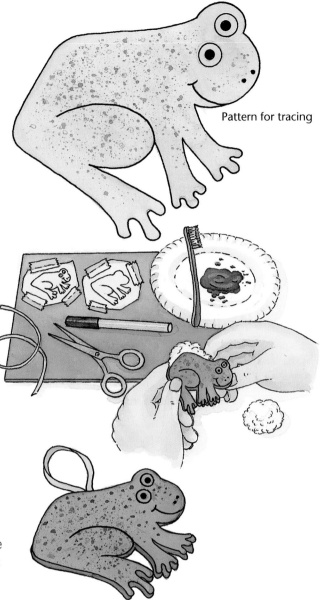

Pattern for tracing

You Will Need:

One sheet of tracing paper
Pencil
Clear tape
Scissors
One 8.5 x 11-inch sheet of green flexible foam
Medium-tip black permanent felt pen
Medium-brown tempera paint or acrylic paint
Small paper plate
Old toothbrush
Hot-glue gun
Cotton balls
5 inches of narrow ribbon, yarn, or twine, shaped
    into a loop

Directions:

1. With tracing paper, trace the pattern on this page twice. Tape the traced shapes to the foam sheet. On one, use black felt-tip pen to add the details (eyes, legs, etc.) and outline the shape. This will be the front of the ornament. The other traced shape will be the back of the ornament. Cut out both shapes.

2. Spread a small amount of brown paint on a paper plate. Press bristles of toothbrush into the paint to coat them. With toothbrush about 2 inches from the cutout of the front of the coquí, scrape your fingernail down the bristles to spatter tiny drops of paint on the coquí. Repeat for the back of the ornament. Set aside and allow to dry for at least one hour.

3. When the paint is dry, lay the front of the coquí down atop the back. Apply hot glue to the inside edge of the back, going 3/4 of the way around it. Press front to back and hold until glue sets. Then gently stuff a few cotton balls inside the pouch you've created. Distribute them evenly to give the coquí a 3-dimensional appearance. Apply glue to the rest of the coquí, but before you press the front to the back, insert the ends of a loop of ribbon, yarn, or twine to make a hanger. Seal edges and hold until dry. Use scissors to trim any excess glue or cotton.

Nativity Diorama

This project makes use of craft materials you may have at home or can find easily in stores. You may make substitutions as desired. For instance, to make the Three Kings' clothes, you may use fabric or felt scraps instead of wired ribbon. You may add angels, townspeople, and other figurines found at Christmas ornament stores or in model train and dollhouse stores. For a uniquely Puerto Rican diorama, use horses instead of camels to accompany the Three Wise Men, and perch a rooster on a nearby fencepost made of Popsicle sticks or twigs.

You Will Need:

Hot-glue gun

Six natural wood doll head beads (18 mm)

Five wooden clothespins, nonspring style, approximately 3.75 inches tall

About eight 8-inch ribbon scraps (wire-edge)

Scissors

Five twist ties or 6-inch scraps of twine or yarn

Three squares of plain white toilet paper

Basket filler straw/shredded paper (enough to fill base of crate when it is stood on its long side)

Empty, small gift box bottom

One sheet brown construction paper or brown preprinted scrapbook paper

Pencil

Clear tape

One sheet green construction paper or green preprinted scrapbook paper

One wooden fruit crate such as from clementine oranges

Thin cardboard to cover bottom of crate

Modeling clay

Assorted plastic farm animals

Directions:

To make the Three Wise Men and Joseph:
With glue gun, glue one doll head bead onto top of a clothespin. Set aside. Fold one 8-inch ribbon strip in half so it is doubled over as two 4-inch strips. Cut small lengthwise slit in center. Slip ribbon over the previously prepared clothespin Wise Man's head. Tie at waist with twist tie or twine/yarn. Repeat these steps with the other two Wise Men.

To make Mary:
With glue gun, glue one doll head bead onto top of a clothespin. Set aside. Fold one 8-inch ribbon strip in half so it is doubled over as two 4-inch strips. Cut small lengthwise slit in center. Slip ribbon over the previously prepared clothespin woman's head. Take a second ribbon strip and drape it over the head of the clothespin, as a scarf and shawl.

To make the Christ child:

Fold over the toilet paper to a single square, triple thickness. Lay it flat in a diamond shape. Fold down the top corner 1 inch. Fold over the left side two-thirds of the way. Fold over the right side two-thirds of the way. Tuck the bottom corner under, and shape bottom into a point to make the Christ child's swaddling clothes. Lay one wooden doll head bead in the opening at the top of the swaddling clothes, and glue it in place. Place a small handful of basket filler in the gift box bottom, and lay the Christ child in it.

To make the palm trees:

Cut a strip of brown paper 6 inches long by 2 inches wide. Roll it around a pencil to shape a tree trunk. Tape the seam closed; remove pencil. Cut a strip of green paper 5.5 inches long by 3.5 inches wide. Roll it around a pencil, green side in; do not tape. Insert one end of green rolled paper into the brown tree trunk. With scissors, cut slits lengthwise down the green roll, until you reach the tree trunk. Fan out "branches" of palm tree, curling some downward. Repeat these steps as desired with slightly shorter strips of brown and green paper to make trees of varying heights.

To assemble the stable:

Glue a sheet of craft paper, thin cardboard, or other plain paper, cut to fit, in bottom of the crate. Stand crate up on one long end. Spread basket filler or shredded paper on floor of crate. Position Mary, Joseph, the Christ child (in the manger), and various animals in the stable. Position the Three Wise Men and their three horses just outside the stable. (Tip: Secure figures to base with a small ball of modeling clay.) Place palm trees on either side of the stable.

Poinsettia Centerpiece

You Will Need:

12 yards of 1.5-inch-wide wire-edged red or
burgundy taffeta ribbon
Scissors
30-gauge floral wire
2 yards of 1.5-inch-wide wire-edged gold
ribbon
Hot-glue gun
Gold glass rochaille beads or other small
gold beads
1.5 yards of 1.5-inch-wide wire-edged
pale yellow taffeta ribbon
9 inches of 1.5-inch-wide wire-edged
green taffeta ribbon
One green styrofoam brick (12 inches by
4 inches by 2 inches)
Two 8-inch green taper candles

Directions:

1. To form first red poinsettia, cut three 6-inch
lengths of red or burgundy ribbon. Cut the ends
of each strip into a point. Lay strips atop one
another, pinch the lengths at the center (use an
accordion fold), and wire the strips together with
floral wire. Fan out the petals into a circle. Set
aside. Next, cut four 8-inch lengths of red or
burgundy ribbon. Cut the ends of each strip into a
point. Lay strips atop one another and pinch the
lengths at the center. Lay the 6-inch petals atop
the 8-inch strips. Wire together and fan out the
petals. Then cut the ends of the gold ribbon into a
point. Lay the red flower atop the gold "leaf" and
wire the "leaf" to the bottom of the red flower.
Place a small circle of hot glue in the center of the
red flower and cover with gold beads. Pat gently.
Shake off any loose beads.

2. Repeat the first step seven more times to form
a total of eight red poinsettias.

3. To form the pale yellow poinsettia, repeat the
first step, substituting pale yellow ribbon for the
red/burgundy and green ribbon for the gold.

4. Position the pale yellow poinsettia in the
middle of the base. Position the red poinsettias to
cover the rest of the base. Place the two green
candles between the center and outer poinsettias,
pressing down into the styrofoam to settle them
securely. After you have all flowers and candles
where you want them, use hot glue to attach the
flowers to the styrofoam base. Allow to dry
before using.

*Caution: Adults should light candles.
Extinguish candles and replace them when they
are 4 inches from base. Do not leave lighted
candles unattended.*

Papier-Mâché Maracas

Use these festive maracas for your own parrandas party!

You Will Need:

Old newspapers for work area

Two small pear-shaped balloons (about 4 inches long when inflated)

6 tablespoons all-purpose flour

1 cup water

Long, thin strips of newspaper (about 6 inches long by 1 inch thick)

Plate

Pencil

Uncooked rice, split peas, small dried beans, or plain large-pearl cous-cous

One cardboard inner core from paper towel roll, cut into two equal lengths

Scissors

Masking tape

1 tablespoon all-purpose flour

3 tablespoons water

Tempera paint or acrylic paint

Paint brushes

Directions:

1. Prepare your work surface by spreading a thick layer of old newspapers over it.

2. Inflate balloons and tie a knot at the end of each. *Do not fully inflate the balloons.*

3. Add the flour to the water, one spoonful at a time, mixing until all lumps have been dissolved. The mixture should form a thin paste. If too thick, add water a teaspoonful at a time; if too thin, add flour in same quantity.

4. Cover the newspaper strips with papier-mâché by pulling each strip through the paste. Lay strips across one balloon until the entire balloon is covered. Cover with a second layer of strips going in the opposite direction. Press down any loose edges. Lay balloon on a plate and set it to dry someplace where it won't be disturbed. Repeat step 4 with the other balloon. Allow at least 24 hours to dry.

5. When balloons are completely dry, use a pencil or other sharp point to pop them. (Make the incision at the base of the balloon, where knot had been tied.) If possible, remove the deflated balloon through the opening of a maraca. Enlarge opening to about the diameter of a penny. Carefully pour about 1 tablespoonful of the rice, peas, beans, or cous-cous into the papier-mâché shell through the opening you made. Give a few shakes to test the tone; if desired, add more grains until you like the way they sound.

6. Take one of the paper towel roll halves, and slit it open lengthwise with scissors. Re-roll the half tightly (about the width of a pencil) to make the maraca handle. Tape the edges and seam. Cover one end of handle with tape. Repeat step 6 to make the second handle.

7. Gently insert the taped end of one handle into the opening of a balloon. Seal the opening with a little papier-mâché paste (made from the additional 1 tablespoon of flour and 3 tablespoons of water) and shredded newspaper. Set the maraca to dry overnight. Repeat step 7 with the other balloon.

8. Paint the maracas and their handles with a base coat of tempera or acrylic paint. Allow to dry overnight. If using a light color, apply a second coat when dry, and allow 24 hours more for drying.

9. Paint on any decorations you choose—stripes, dots, faces, flowers, or other details. Allow to dry completely.

10. Shake, rattle, and roll!

Carols

"Villancico Yaucano"
Words and Music by Amaury Veray Torregrosa
Copyright © 1978 Southern Music Publishing Co., Inc.
All Rights Administered by Peer International Corporation
International Copyright Secured. All Rights Reserved.

Villancico Yaucano

(Christmas Carol from Yauco) Amaury Veray

Moderato

1. Qui - sie - ra Ni - ño be - sar - te   y San Jo - sé no me
   Ha na - ci - do en un por - tal   lle - ni - to de te - la-
2. Yo soy un po - bre yau - ca - no   que ven - go de Yau - co a-
   Ya lo sa - bes Ni - ño her - mo - so   soy del pue - blo del ca-

de - ja   di - ce que te ha - ré llo - rar;   ver - dad que aún a-
ra - ñas   en - tre la mu - la y el buey   el Re - den - tor
quí   y a mi Ni - ño Dios le trai - go   un ga - llo qui-
fé   por si quie - res dos sa - qui - tos   tam - bién yo te

sí me de - jas.   1. En Be - lén to - can a   fue - go
de las al - mas.   2. Yo soy Juan el ver - du -   re - ro
quí - ri - quí.   3. Al Ni - ño re - cién na -   ci - do
los trae - ré.

1 y 2 (2da vez al %)

Del por - tal sa - le u - na lla - ma;   es u - na es - tre - lla del - cie - lo
que ven - go de la mon - ta - ña   y te trai - go vian - das bue - nas
to - dos le o - fre - cen un don

que ha ca - í - do en - tre las   pa - jas.   3. Yo co - mo no ten - go   na - da
des - de mi hu - mil - de ca -   ba - ña.

le o - frez - co mi co - ra - zón.

1. I'd like, Child, to kiss you
And Saint Joseph doesn't let me
He says I'll make you cry
Isn't it true that even so you let me?

He has been born in a stable
Full of spider webs
Between the mule and the ox
The Redeemer of souls.

In Bethlehem they cry fire
From the stable rises a flame
It is a star from the sky
That has fallen in the straw.

2. I am a poor Yaucano
I come from Yauco to here
And to the Baby Jesus I bring
A qui-qui-ri-qui rooster.

You already know it, beautiful Child
I am from the coffee town
In case you want two little sacks
I will bring them to you too.

I am Juan the greengrocer
Who comes from the mountain
And I bring you delicious viands
From my humble hut.

To the newborn Child
Everyone offers a gift
I, as I have nothing ...
I offer Him my heart!

Si Me Dan Pasteles

(If You Give Me Pasteles) Traditional Puerto Rican Carol

Si me dan   paste-les, dénmelos ca - lientes, que pasteles frí - os empachan la   gente.
If you give me paste-les, give them to me hot, because cold   paste-les make people sick.

Si me dan   a - rroz no me den cu - chara,   que mamá me dijo que se lo lle-vara.
If you give me rice, do not give me a   spoon, because mama told me to take the rice to her.

RECIPES

Candied Plantains

4 large, ripe plantains (skin should be partially black)
2 quarts water
2 tbsp. salt
1 stick of butter, melted
3 tbsp. brown sugar
ground cinnamon

Peel plantains. Make 3 diagonal slashes on each side of plantains. Combine water and salt in a large pot. Soak plantains in salted water for 30 minutes. Remove from water.

Preheat oven to 350 °F. In a small saucepan, melt butter. Spray a shallow baking dish with cooking spray, and place plantains in dish. Brush the plantains with half the melted butter. Sprinkle half the brown sugar over the plantains. Bake for 30 minutes. Gently turn plantains over, brush with the remaining butter, and sprinkle remainder of brown sugar over top. Lightly sprinkle cinnamon atop plantains. Bake for 30 minutes or until tender. (If plantains dry out during baking, brush with additional melted butter.)

Serves 4.

Coconut Pudding (Tembleque)

4 cups canned, unsweetened
  coconut milk
1/2 cup cornstarch
1/4 tsp. salt

1/2 cup sugar
1 tbsp. orange blossom water
  (optional)
ground cinnamon

In small bowl, combine 1/2 cup of the coconut milk with the cornstarch and salt. Mix well, until all lumps have dissolved. Set aside.

In a 4-quart saucepan, combine the remainder of the coconut milk with the sugar and the orange blossom water (if using). Bring to a boil, stirring constantly. As soon as mixture begins to boil, gradually add the cornstarch mixture, whisking constantly. Reduce heat to low. Cook 5 minutes more, stirring constantly.

Remove pan from heat. Pour the mixture into an aluminum mold. Cool to room temperature, then cover with plastic wrap and refrigerate at least 3 hours. When ready to serve, unmold the pudding and sprinkle cinnamon lightly over the top.

Serves 4.

Chilled Tropical Salad

1/2 cup olive oil
1/4 cup red wine vinegar
1/4 tsp. ground white pepper
1 tbsp. sugar
1/4 tsp. lime juice
1/2 tsp. salt
1/2 head cabbage, core removed

1 cucumber, peeled and thinly sliced
1 green pepper, seeded and thinly
   sliced
5 medium-small onions, peeled and
   thinly sliced
6 radishes, thinly sliced
1 large, ripe avocado

Combine the olive oil, vinegar, pepper, sugar, lime juice, and salt in a mixing bowl. Stir well, then set dressing aside.

Shred the cabbage and place in a large mixing bowl. Add the sliced cucumber, green pepper, onions, and radishes.

Peel the avocado and slice into thick slices. Add to salad.

Pour dressing over salad. Mix thoroughly. Refrigerate at least 2 hours before serving.

Serves 6.

Spice Cake

1 3/4 cups all-purpose flour
1 tbsp. baking powder
1/8 tsp. salt
3/4 tsp. ground cinnamon
1/4 tsp. ground nutmeg
1/4 tsp. ground cloves

1 cup raisins or currants
1 1/2 cups brown sugar
   (firmly packed)
1/2 cup very cold water
2 eggs
1/4 lb. butter, melted

Preheat oven to 350 °F.

Spray a 9-inch x 5-inch x 2 3/4-inch aluminum pan with cooking spray. Coat the sprayed surface with flour.

Into a mixing bowl, sift together the flour, baking powder, salt, cinnamon, nutmeg, and cloves.

Measure out 1/2 cup of the flour mixture. (Set the rest aside.) Use the 1/2 cup flour to dredge the raisins or currants. Set raisins/currants aside.

To the reserved flour mixture in the mixing bowl, gradually add the brown sugar, cold water, eggs, and melted butter. Mix well. Add the dredged raisins or currants, mixing just enough to combine.

Spoon batter into the greased and floured pan. Bake about 1 hour, until toothpick inserted into cake comes out clean. Cool for 5 minutes on a wire rack. Remove from pan and serve warm or at room temperature.

Serves 6.

Stewed Shrimp

2 pounds fresh or newly defrosted
   shrimp
2 quarts water
2 bay leaves
4 black peppercorns
4 tbsp. salt
1 oz. salt pork
2 oz. lean cured ham, diced
1 onion, peeled and chopped
1 green pepper, seeded and chopped
3 sweet chili peppers, seeded and
   chopped

2 cloves garlic, peeled and chopped
6 fresh cilantro leaves, chopped, or
   1/8 tsp. dried cilantro
1 lb. potatoes, peeled and cubed
1 28-oz. can whole peeled tomatoes
1/4 cup tomato sauce
1 tsp. brown sugar
1 tsp. red wine vinegar
1 tsp. capers
2 tsp. salt
3 whole bay leaves
1 tsp. lime juice

Wash the shrimp thoroughly. In a medium saucepan, bring to a boil 2 quarts of water, 2 bay leaves, 4 black peppercorns, and 4 tbsp. salt. Add the shrimp. Reduce heat to low and simmer for 5 minutes. Drain shrimp. Remove shells and devein. Refrigerate until ready to use.

Score the salt pork, cutting most of the way through but not all the way to the rind. In a heavy soup pot, quickly brown the salt pork and ham. Remove salt pork and discard it. Reduce heat to low.

Add to the kettle the chopped onion, green pepper, chili peppers, garlic, and cilantro. Sauté for 10 minutes, stirring occasionally.

Add the remainder of the ingredients except for the shrimp and lime juice. Rapidly bring to a boil. Reduce heat to medium. Cover pot and cook for 30 minutes, or until potatoes are tender. Add the poached shrimp and lime juice. Mix together, and cook, uncovered, until sauce thickens.

Serves 6.

Rice Fritters

Rice mixture:
1 cup cooked white rice
1 egg, beaten
1/4 tsp. salt
1 tbsp. milk
1 tbsp. sugar

Flour mixture:
2/3 cup all-purpose flour
1/4 tsp. salt
1 tsp. baking powder
1/2 cup milk
1 1/2 tbsp. sugar
1 tsp. vanilla extract
vegetable oil

In a large mixing bowl, combine white rice, egg, 1/4 tsp. salt, 1 tbsp. milk, and 1 tbsp. sugar. Mix well. Set aside.

In a separate bowl, mix flour, 1/4 tsp. salt, 1 tsp. baking powder, 1/2 cup milk, 1 1/2 tbsp. sugar, and vanilla extract.

Add the flour mixture to the rice mixture, stirring well.

Pour oil 1 to 2 inches deep in a frying pan; heat. Drop rice mixture by tablespoonfuls into the hot oil. Fry fritters until golden brown. Remove with a slotted spoon and drain on a plate covered with paper towels.

Serves 4.

Pasteles

Filling (el relleno):
2 lbs. lean fresh pork
2 cloves garlic
1 tbsp. fresh oregano leaves, chopped
3 fresh cilantro leaves or a pinch of dried cilantro
1 tbsp. salt
1 onion, chopped
1 green pepper, chopped
1 lb. lean cured ham
30 green olives stuffed with pimentos, chopped
2 tbsp. capers
4 tbsp. annatto oil*
1 cup water

Paste:
15 very green bananas
1 tsp. salt
2 cups lukewarm water
6 lbs. taro root (*yautia*)
2 cups milk
8 oz. annatto oil*
2 tbsp. salt

Wrapping:
6 dozen large, wide plantain leaves or parchment paper
vegetable oil
one roll of butcher's twine
20 cups of water
3 tbsp. salt
* *recipe for annatto oil follows*

Filling (el relleno):
Cut fresh pork into small cubes. Set aside in a mixing bowl. Crush the garlic, oregano, cilantro, and salt in a mortar, and mix with the pork. Add the onion and green pepper.

Cut the cured ham into small cubes and add to mixing bowl. Blend ingredients thoroughly. Mix in the olives and capers. Stir in the annatto oil; blend well. Place the mixture in a large saucepan, add the cup of water, and cook over medium heat 30 minutes, stirring occasionally. Remove from heat; transfer to a storage container and refrigerate while you prepare the paste.

Paste:
Peel the bananas. Combine 1 tsp. salt with the 2 cups water; stir to dissolve. Rinse the peeled bananas in the salt water. Discard salt water, and cut each banana in half. Wash the taro roots and cut each in half. Coarsely grate the taro roots and bananas into a large mixing bowl. Stir in the milk; mix thoroughly. Blend in the annatto oil and the 2 tbsp. salt. Set aside.

Wrapping:
Use a knife or cooking shears to shape the plantain leaves into squares no smaller than 10 inches and no larger than 14 inches. (Note: If you cannot get plantain leaves, you may substitute parchment paper squares of equivalent size.) Wipe leaves with a damp paper towel or damp clean cloth.

Remove the filling from the refrigerator. Lay one plantain leaf or parchment paper square flat. Spread some oil on the center of the leaf or paper, using the back of a spoon dipped in vegetable oil. Place 2 to 3 tbsp. of the paste in the center of the leaf or paper. Spread the paste out evenly and thinly so it is almost transparent. Paste should extend to within an inch of each edge of the square.

Place 2 to 3 tbsp. of the filling to the left of the center of the paste on the leaf or paper. (Do not spread it out as much as the paste.) Fold over the half of the leaf or paper that has no filling so that it covers the other half. You will then have a border of plantain leaf or parchment paper on all 4 sides of the rectangle. Fold these sides over too. Lay down another plantain leaf or parchment paper square and wrap the first leaf or parchment paper square and pastel in this. Repeat the process once more. Wrap the pastel bundle in 3 places with butcher's twine and tie securely.

In a large, deep pot (8 quarts or more), bring 20 cups of water to a boil. Add 3 tbsp. salt. Gently place 12 pasteles in the water. Boil, covered, for 30 minutes, then turn pasteles over and cook for 20 to 30 minutes more. Remove from water, and repeat the cooking process with the next batch of pasteles.

When all pasteles are done, unwrap and serve while still hot.

Serves 12 to 18 (yields 36 pasteles).

Annatto Oil*

8 tbsp. vegetable oil
8 tbsp. annatto seeds

Combine oil and annatto seeds in a small saucepan. Cook over medium heat until the seeds begin to color the oil a deep orange-red. As soon as the color starts to change to gold, remove pan from heat promptly. Strain through a fine-mesh wire strainer; discard seeds. Store oil in a glass jar with tight-fitting lid. Oil will keep for several months if stored in a cool, dry place.

Yield: 8 tbsp.

used in Pasteles recipe, pages 75-76

Glossary

adobo *(ah DOH boh)* a seasoning mixture rubbed into meat before roasting. Adobo is made with crushed peppercorns, oregano, salt, olive oil, and lime juice or vinegar.

aguinaldo *(AH gee NAHL doh)* a type of traditional Puerto Rican Christmas carol based on old Spanish folk songs.

annatto *(uh NAT oh* or *uh NAH toh)* an orange-red dye obtained from the waxy pulp surrounding the seeds of a small tree native to tropical America, used for coloring textiles, butter, cheese, varnishes, and lacquers.

asalto *(ah SAHL toh)* a noisy, surprise musical visit of Christmas carolers at someone's home during the night: a surprise parranda. See also *parranda*.

bomba *(BOHM bah)* a type of folk dance music with African roots featuring an improvised interchange between dancers and drummers.

Borikén *(boh ree KAYN)* the name given to Puerto Rico by Taíno Indians. It means "Great Land of the Valiant and Noble Lord."

Borinquen *(boh reen KAYN)* a popular name for Puerto Rico.

carrozas *(kah ROH zahs)* decorated automobiles used in festivals or parades.

cascabeles *(KAHS kah bel ays)* "jingle bells."

coquí *(koh KEE)* a small tree frog found in Puerto Rico that sounds a clear, musical note in the evening.

coquito *(koh KEE toh)* a traditional holiday drink made of rum and coconut milk.

cuatro *(KWAHT roh)* a 10-stringed guitarlike instrument unique to Puerto Rico.

décima *(DAY see mah)* an ancient form of Spanish poetry consisting of 10 lines of 8 syllables each, with a complex rhyme scheme.

Encendidos de la Navidad *(ehn sehn DEE dohs day lah nah vee DAHD)* lighting celebrations that include the turning on of Christmas lights, the lighting of municipal Christmas trees, and performances.

Feliz Navidad *(fay LEES nah vee DAHD)* "Merry Christmas."

gandules *(gahn DOO lays)* pigeon peas; served in traditional Puerto Rican dishes.

güiro *(GWEE roh)* a notched gourd played by drawing a stick or forklike scraper across it.

jíbaro *(HEE bah roh)* a person of rural Hispanic Puerto Rican origin.

lechón asado *(lay CHOHN ah SAH doh)* barbecued or roasted whole pig.

lechonera *(lay chohn EH rah)* a restaurant that specializes in *lechón asado*.

máscara *(MAHS kah rah)* a mask; a person wearing a disguise or mask.

mestizo *(mehs TEE zoh)* a person of mixed Spanish and American Indian or African ancestry.

misa de aguinaldo *(MEE sah day AH gee NAHL doh)* a festive Mass celebrated at a Catholic church at dawn on each of the nine days preceding Christmas Eve.

misa de gallo *(MEE sah day GY oh)* a solemn but festive Mass celebrated at midnight on Christmas Eve.

nacimiento *(nah see mee EHN toh)* nativity scene.

Navidad *(nah vee DAHD)* Christmas Day.

Nochebuena *(noh chay BWAY nah)* Christmas Eve.

octavas *(ohk TAH vahs),* **las,** a celebration beginning January 9 and lasting eight days giving praise to the Three Kings and commemorating the adoration of the baby Jesus. **Las octavitas** *(ohk tah VEE tahs)* are eight additional days of devotion following las octavas.

parranda *(pah RHAHN dah)* a holiday activity in which a group of people goes door to door singing Christmas carols, often accompanied by instruments. See also *asalto; trulla*.

pastel *(pah STEHL)* a tamalelike, boiled meat-filled dough roll.

pava *(PAH vah)* a straw hat often worn by *jíbaros*.

petate *(pay TAH tay)* a sleeping mat woven from the fronds of the brittle thatch, or broom, palm.

plantain *(PLAN tuhn)* a bananalike fruit, longer and more starchy than the banana, usually eaten cooked.

santero *(san TAY roh)* a person who carves figures of saints called *santos*.

santo *(SAHN toh)* a carved saint figure.

seis bombeao *(SAYS bom bay AH oh)* a popular dance done at parrandas and other holiday get-togethers that combines words and movement.

sofrito *(soh FREE toh)* a green or orange-red seasoning made of onions, garlic, coriander, and peppers blended together. Sofrito is the basis for many Puerto Rican soups, stews, and rice dishes.

Taíno *(ty EE noh)* the original inhabitants of Puerto Rico.

tembleque *(tehm BLAY kay)* a firm and shaky coconut pudding.

tostones *(toh STOHN ays)* a side dish of fried, mashed, and refried green plantain.

trulla *(TROO yah)* a small band of carolers who arrive at a friend's home unannounced.

villancico *(vee yan SEE koh)* a type of religious Christmas carol related to the story of the Nativity.

Index

Page numbers in *italic* type refer to illustrations.

Acknowledgments

Cover	© Stone from Getty Images; © Suzanne Murphy-Larronde, DDB Stock Photo	23-24	© Antonio Amador, Pro Pix Brochures
2	© Ricardo Medina	25	© Suzanne Murphy-Larronde, DDB Stock Photo
5	© Antonio Amador, Pro Pix Brochures	26	AP/Wide World
6	© Bob Krist, Corbis	27	© Ricardo Medina
7	© Robert Fried, DDB Stock Photo	29-30	© Antonio Amador, Pro Pix Brochures
9	© Bob Krist, Puerto Rico Tourism Company; © Charles O'Rear, Corbis	33	© Bob Krist, Puerto Rico Tourism Company
10	AP/Wide World	34-39	© Antonio Amador, Pro Pix Brochures
11	© Corbis	40-44	© Ricardo Medina
12	© Suzanne Murphy-Larronde, DDB Stock Photo; © Bob Krist, Corbis	50	© Antonio Amador, Pro Pix Brochures
14	© Antonio Amador, Pro Pix Brochures	52-54	AP/Wide World
16	© Suzanne Murphy-Larronde, DDB Stock Photo	56	© Suzanne Murphy-Larronde, DDB Stock Photo
17-19	© Ricardo Medina	57	AP/Wide World
20	© Antonio Amador, Pro Pix Brochures	58-59	© Antonio Amador, Pro Pix Brochures
22	© Suzanne Murphy-Larronde, DDB Stock Photo; © Stephanie Maze, Corbis	60	© Suzanne Murphy-Larronde, DDB Stock Photo

Craft Illustrations: Eileen Mueller Neill*
Recipe Cards: Eileen Mueller Neill*
Advent Calendar: © Antonio Amador, Pro Pix Brochures
Advent Calendar Illustrations: Eileen Mueller Neill*
All entries marked with an asterisk (*) denote illustrations created exclusively for World Book, Inc.